Teaching Religion in School

Jean L. Holm

SACRED
PLACES

Oxford Studies in Education

Teaching religion in school

Oxford studies in education

Teaching religion in school
A practical approach

Jean L. Holm

Principal Lecturer in Religious Studies
Homerton College

Oxford University Press 1975

Oxford University Press, Ely House, London W1

Glasgow New York Toronto Melbourne Wellington
Cape Town Ibadan Nairobi Dar es Salaam Lusaka Addis Ababa
Delhi Bombay Calcutta Madras Karachi Lahore Dacca
Kuala Lumpur Singapore Hong Kong Tokyo

Printed in Great Britain by
Butler & Tanner Ltd., Frome and London

Cover photo by William Palmer

Preface

This book is offered to non-specialist teachers, to students preparing for teaching and to specialist teachers who may be wondering about the direction in which the subject is moving. Its thinking is the result of wrestling with questions about the nature and aims of religious education with generations of students and practising teachers on in-service courses, and I should like to record my gratitude to them for the stimulus they provided.

I have attempted the daunting task of looking at religious education across the entire school age range, and neither the book nor individual chapters are neatly divided according to age groups. This is a recognition both of the increasing interest being taken by teachers in age groups other than their own and of the need, particularly in R.E., for an understanding of the subject as a whole if any section of it is to be taught effectively.

There is no longer a standard terminology for describing schools. Where reference is made to First, Middle and Upper school and senior pupils the age groups are 5–8, 9–13, 13+ and 15+.

The chart of teaching units suggests topics which might be treated in a reasonably systematic way. It should not be interpreted to mean that this is all that religious education consists of.

I acknowledge gratefully the help I have received from Charles Bailey and David Stacey who read and commented on chapters 1–3, from Michael Anderson, Frances Findlay and Jane Mayles who advised on the choice of children's literature, from representatives of the major non-Christian religions—Rabbi D. S. Charing (Judaism), Mr. R. El Droubie (Islam), Mr. R. Webb (Buddhism), Mrs. P. M. Wylam (Manjeet Kaur) (Sikhism), and Swami Yogeshananda (Hinduism)—who checked and advised on the references to their faiths. I am also grateful to the Christian Education Movement for allowing me to use material from articles I had written for their Primary R. E. Resource Material Scheme.

November 1974   J.L.H.

Contents

Contents

1

Changes in direction

This book is called *Teaching Religion in School* because it explores what is involved in helping pupils to understand, by the time they leave secondary school, what religion is and what it would mean to take a religion seriously.

As most readers will not have experienced this kind of R.E. themselves at school, and few will have taught it, it may be helpful to trace briefly the two changes in direction which the subject has taken in recent years.

The first change came in the 1960s in response to research being done by educational psychologists. They asked questions like 'How do children learn?' and 'How are concepts formed?' The results of their research presented a challenge to the familiar form of much of the curriculum, especially in the primary school. In religious education this challenge was reinforced when a number of pieces of research (University of Sheffield Institute of Education, *Religious Education in Secondary Schools*, Nelson, 1961; Harold Loukes, *Teenage Religion*, S.C.M. Press, 1961; Ronald Goldman, *Religious Thinking from Childhood to Adolescence*, Routledge and Kegan Paul, 1964; K. E. Hyde, *Religious Learning in Adolescence,* Oliver and Boyd, 1965; Edwin Cox, *Sixth Form Religion*, S.C.M. Press, 1967) revealed just how little the pupils remembered of what they had been taught and, more important, how distorted was their understanding of what they did remember.

The work of the educational psychologists showed us how important the child's experience is in the process of learning. Emphasis was therefore put on relating the curriculum to life, and in religious education the traditional Bible-centred syllabuses gave way to problem-centred discussion in the secondary school (largely under the influence of the writings of Harold Loukes) and to life-themes in the primary school (largely under the influence of the writings of Ronald Goldman). Expressions like 'child-centred' and 'life-centred' became popular and in many schools the familiar content of religious education disappeared almost entirely. Personal relationships, the community and problems in society became for many teachers the significant element in R.E.

The R.E. of the sixties looked so different from the traditional Bible-centred R.E. that many of its critics attacked it as 'humanist', but it still really belonged to what one can call the confessional approach. It took for granted that the teachers—class teachers in the primary school as well as R.E. specialists in the secondary school—would be committed to the Christian faith themselves and would help pupils towards a similar commitment. This was obvious in the *Readiness for Religion* life-themes edited by Ronald Goldman. Exploration of the life of the shepherd led up to Jesus the Good Shepherd, exploration of the properties and importance of light led up to Jesus as the Light of the World. For secondary pupils the discussions about personal relationships or choosing a job or hunger or homelessness tended to be supported by reference to the teaching of Jesus and other passages from the Bible. The justification for this experiential approach, with or without material from the Bible, was that the values which were being presented to the pupils reflected Christian theology and expressed it in non-theological terms.

A very different understanding of religious education emerged in the seventies. This second change in direction came largely in response to the kind of questions which were being asked by the philosophers of education, such as 'What should the purpose of education be?' and 'How do you justify the different elements in the school curriculum?' They claimed that a general education for all children (to be distinguished from additional specialist courses) should be based on an understanding of what it is that makes us distinctively human.

In this country it is the work of Paul Hirst and Richard Peters that has had most influence on educational thinking. Less well known in Britain are the writings of the American philosopher of education, Philip Phenix. Phenix considered that what characterised human beings was that they were 'essentially creatures who have the power to express meanings' (*Realms of Meaning*, McGraw Hill, 1964, p.5). He suggested that there were six realms of meaning, six distinctive ways in which man comes to terms with and makes sense of his experience, and that therefore some initiation into these six realms was essential for the development of whole persons.

The realms of meaning that Phenix identified are:

1   *Symbolics* Neutral tools of communication, e.g., language, mathematics and symbolic forms such as gestures and rituals.
2   *Empirics* Factual descriptions of the world, e.g., the sciences of the physical world and of living things (including man).
3   *Esthetics* The arts, e.g., music, the visual arts, the arts of movement and literature.
4   *Synnoetics* Phenix coined this term to express the kind of direct awareness we have of people as persons. This realm of meaning is concerned with our knowledge of persons and with our understanding of what it is to be a person, in relation to other persons. It includes aspects of literature and religion and is obviously very important in religious education.
5   *Ethics* Meanings that express obligations.
6   *Synoptics* Phenix put history, philosophy and religion under this heading. What they have in common is that each constructs a coherent pattern which includes all the other realms of meaning. Religion, for example, is concerned with the *whole* of life, seen from a religious perspective.

To quote Phenix again, 'The logic of the synoptic disciplines places them last in order, because they depend upon all the other realms for their materials' (op. cit., p.281). This does not mean that religious education should be postponed till the fifth or sixth form of the secondary school, but it does mean that we must not expect pupils in the earlier years to have any kind of complete understanding of what religion is. And it also means that we have to analyse religion into its different elements and so structure our religious education that over the years the pupils are able to build up their knowledge of it and eventually acquire a reasonably comprehensive understanding of what religion as a whole is.

What we have called the religious education of the seventies resulted from taking seriously the questions asked by both the educational psychologists and the educational philosophers. It took into account the emotional and intellectual development of children and the ways in which they learn. It also set out to provide a valid and essential educational experience for *all* children and to contribute to their full development as persons, whether their background, or later commitment, was Christian, Jewish, Muslim, Hindu, Sikh or humanist.

If religious education is to provide a good educational experience for all pupils irrespective of their religious (or non-religious) background, then it is quite obvious that it can no longer be confessional, that is, concerned to initiate pupils into a particular religious faith or to help them to grow in such a faith. That is the function of the religious community and of the family—Christian, Jewish, Muslim or whatever.

After the first change in direction, in the sixties, it became common to talk about the task of R.E., at least in the secondary school, as helping pupils to 'find a faith to live by'. This expression tended to be used by teachers who advocated what was then called 'open-ended R.E.' (an unfortunate description which caused much misunderstanding). However, even though this policy represented a shift away from the explicitly evangelistic aims of traditional R.E., it still involved putting Christianity—its values rather than its beliefs—before pupils with the intention of letting them choose for themselves. In the sixties this virtually meant choosing between a religious and a non-religious way of life, between Christianity and humanism. In one sense this is still a very important choice for young people as they move towards adult life, but the choice can only be made when the pupils have studied with some seriousness the nature of religious and non-religious systems of belief and the grounds which men of good-will and sincerity on both sides find convincing. The problem-centred syllabuses of the R.E. of the sixties provided a quite inadequate basis for choice; there are no problems in society—from abortion to war, from the use of money to crime and punishment—to which all Christians suggest one solution and all humanists another.

One of the results of the more extensive teaching of world religions in recent years has been that many teachers just assumed that the choice was now automatically extended to a larger number of options. But it is not the task of the school to present all the major religions and non-religious systems of belief to the pupils so that they can choose which one they want. The assumption that religions are like detergents or instant coffee, and we choose the brand that appeals to us most, betrays a lack of understanding of the nature of religion. Religions are closely interwoven with the cultures in which they are embedded. Our whole outlook on life is shaped by the religion within which we grow up, and a complete shift of focus—world view, culture, way of life—is required if we 'adopt' another religion. Some people are converted from one religion to another, but it is never more than a tiny minority of the total membership of a religion. Those who take such a tremendous step do so for a complex variety of reasons, but seldom because they have undertaken a comparative study of religions course.

What is involved in teaching religious education after its second change of direction is the subject of the rest of this book, but one important effect of the new approach can be mentioned here—its implications for teachers.

Traditional R.E. aimed to communicate the Christian faith. As this can logically be done only by those who are already within the faith, the assumption was that teachers would be Christians. At the secondary level specialist teachers were, almost without exception, members of the Christian Church, and it was a common practice for heads to invite teachers of other subjects who happened to be Christians to help out with R.E. Primary teachers were however in a quite different situation. Whatever their own convictions they were expected to follow Christian Agreed Syllabuses, and although there was a conscience clause for teachers many hesitated to invoke it because of all the complications it would cause in a sector of the education system that was based on class teaching and integrated work.

In the R.E. of the sixties the situation became completely confused. On the one hand, some people assumed that religious education was really moral education and any teacher could, with a good conscience, teach life-themes in the primary school and run discussions on problems in society in the secondary school. On the other hand, it was pointed out that not only does it require a much more profound and comprehensive knowledge of the Bible to be able to use biblical material in life-themes, but if teachers were to be able to press through to the 'ultimate meaning' behind the problems in society or to use life-themes as 'implicit religion', they also needed a profound understanding of Christian theology.

In the religious education of the seventies the ability to teach the subject no longer depends on the teacher's own convictions. He may be a Christian, he may belong to one of the other faiths, he may be a humanist. Or he may himself be searching and so not come into any of these categories. What makes a good teacher of religious education is what makes a good teacher of any subject—the professional qualities of conscientiousness and integrity, sensitivity to other people and concern for the pupils, a real interest in the questions with which his subject deals and a determination to acquire the knowledge needed to teach it.

This last point must not be overlooked, because religious education now makes greater demands on the teacher in terms of knowledge than ever before, though it is comparable to the kind of knowledge needed for other subjects—it can be learned; it doesn't depend on personal faith.

If the role of religious education is seen as educational—providing a good educational experience for all the pupils in a school, then there is no need for a conscience clause for teachers or pupils. Both are engaged in an objective study of religion; they are not assumed to be committed to any religious position.

Where the objective approach has been tried in middle and secondary schools the pupils' response has been most encouraging. They seem to have been freed from the constraints which made them resent the subject. For young people are interested in religion and in man's search for meaning, and when they are no longer on the defensive against what they regard as the teacher's vested interest in Christianity they are willing to enter into the study of religion in a much more co-operative way.

2

What is religion?

We have said that the aim of religious education is to help pupils to understand what religion is and what it would mean to take a religion seriously. But what is religion?

Attempts at defining it are always unsatisfactory. One definition that has been offered is 'belief in a supreme Being or Beings', but that excludes Theravada Buddhism which is non-theistic and it would clearly be ridiculous to say that this form of Buddhism is not a religion. Another definition that has been tried is 'commitment to a set of beliefs by which one lives and for which one is prepared to make great sacrifices', but this would include Marxism and no Marxist would want his beliefs and life style described as religious. Yet a third definition—'that which is our deepest concern' or 'that which we value most'—embraces absolutely everyone, including the atheist. It makes religion synonymous with being human, and although it can be very useful within a religion for describing what a religious perspective on life involves, it fails as a general definition of religion because it evacuates the word of any distinctive meaning.

However, although a satisfactory definition of religion eludes us we can recognise it and we can study it.

Religion has always been an important phenomenon of human experience. It has in fact been a universal phenomenon. As far back as we have evidence of man's thinking we find evidence of religion in one form or another. There seems to be implanted deep in man a need to make sense of his world, to affirm that there is a purpose in the universe that is not of man's making, that the structure of reality is something to which man belongs rather than something which belongs to him.

A religion provides a coherent interpretation of the whole of human life and experience, and it also involves a way of life that is based on that interpretation. Religions suggest answers to the ultimate questions which man asks about his existence. Ultimate questions are the kind of questions to which there are no definitive answers in the human sciences, questions like 'Who am I?', 'What is man?', 'Who is my neighbour?', 'Is there any meaning in life?', 'Is death the end?', 'How do I come to terms with evil and suffering?' All these questions are about meaning. They are concerned with the meaning of man's existence, his relationship with others, his relationship with the natural world.

A religion's answers to these questions can be found in its formulated beliefs, but a religion is much more than just a set of carefully expressed beliefs—in spite of the tendency in this country, especially within the education system, to discuss it as if it were entirely an intellectual matter. In fact ordinary members of any religion will be found to have only the haziest knowledge of the belief system to which they are committed. Any comprehensive knowledge of a religion's beliefs and their relationship to each other is usually the preserve of the professionals—the teachers and the guardians of the faith.

But even if the ordinary person cannot give a coherent exposition of his religion's beliefs they are indirectly related to his life through the many different aspects of religion—through worship and rites and customs, through the festivals that mark his year, through the sacred writings he reads or hears, through the code of ethics he is expected to observe, through the institutions and communities and traditions to which he belongs. Together these make up the coherent interpretation of human life and experience which a religion offers, and they provide a framework for the life of the believer.

This complexity means that if our pupils are to achieve any adequate understanding of the nature of religion they will have to study with some care the different aspects which are involved. For example, a religion doesn't exist in a vacuum. It exists within a particular society. It affects that society and it is in turn affected by it. Islam is recognisably the same religion wherever we meet it but there are clear differences in the people's practice and understanding of it in such countries as Libya, Egypt, Turkey and the Lebanon. In the same way Christianity has taken different forms in Argentina, Ulster, South Africa, Holland, Italy and the U.S.A. (Anyone who is familiar with either of these religions will immediately want to protest, justifiably, that the religion is not homogeneous even within any one of these countries.) Any study of a religion must therefore include a consideration of sociological factors—the social institutions it has developed and its relationship with the society within which it exists.

Religions also exist in time. A religion is not static, it changes and develops. So another element in our study will be history—the factors which have affected religions and the response they have made to those factors. This aspect of the study of religion was included in the older Agreed Syllabuses but the form it took—working through the history of Israel and of the early Church—was not the most effective way of helping pupils to appreciate change and development in religion. There is neither the need nor the time to engage in a long chronological study of any religion, and for First and Middle school children, who have not yet developed a sense of history, it would be a fruitless exercise; rather it is important to focus attention on selected periods in a religion's development. Our aim is not to teach the history of the major religions so much as to enable our pupils to understand how religions develop historically.

Sacred writings are another aspect of religion which must come into our study. They play an important role in each of the major living faiths, and even in religions that have no scriptures as such, e.g., primal religions, there is a tradition of stories, songs, rites, etc., which have been handed down from one generation to another. But not only do sacred writings play a different role in each religion, they also consist of very different kinds of literature. These differences are found within most of the Scriptures as well as between them. The Christian Scriptures, for instance, include letters, hymns, prayers, ancient court chronicles, sagas, etc. The understanding of sacred writings at anything other than a purely superficial level will therefore demand the ability to recognize and handle different kinds of literature.

The beliefs of a religion are expressed also in its code of ethics—the obligations a man has to his fellow man. What any community accepts as right and wrong will be directly related to what it believes about the nature of man and his relationship to the natural world. Morality has been a prominent element in both traditional R.E. and the R.E. of the sixties but the emphasis was put on the pupils' morality. The aim now is to enable the pupils to explore and understand the relationship between belief and ethics. This is not an abdication of responsibility for the moral development of the pupils. Religious education has a contribution to make to that as have other aspects of the curriculum. It is rather a recognition of the distinctive task of R.E. (See chapter 17).

Although there is no such thing as a religion without its social aspect, reflected in communities and institutions and traditions, a religion is made up of individual believers with their fears and their hopes and their longings and their relationship to the object of their worship. A study of religion cannot therefore be complete without serious consideration of the nature of faith, and this will involve some understanding of the psychology of religion.

Some form of worship or mediation, whether private or communal, is a feature of every religion, but it takes different forms in different faiths and it certainly does not mean the same thing in each religion. So again in religious education we shall be concerned not, as in the past, to encourage our pupils to worship, but rather to help them to understand what worship means in the life of the adherent of a living religion (See chapter 15).

Finally, each religion has its pattern of customs and rituals, e.g., the rites of passage, conventions about food, marriage, etc., which form a supportive framework for the life of the believer. These are the things that are 'just there', that are taken for granted. They provide security in times of crisis as well as giving the members of a community a sense of solidarity, of belonging. In any culture there will be many people for whom such practices, especially those relating to birth, marriage and death, are felt in some way to be important long after they themselves have ceased to make any overt confession of faith. The boundary line between religious practices and practices which are not religious is a very blurred one, and an understanding of that fact will be part of what we shall want our pupils to gain from their study in this area.

It will be obvious from the above that a considerable degree of maturity is required in order to achieve such a complex understanding of the nature of religion. The aim of religious education is therefore something to be completely achieved only in the later years of the secondary school; it is the goal at the end of the journey and not the road by which the pupils travel. This is why we need a structure within the subject which will enable us to lay the right kind of foundations and gradually build up a comprehensive understanding of religion.

Although our aim in religious education is to help pupils to under- stand the nature of religion, there is a sense in which there is no such thing as religion. We cannot isolate something called religion and study it. Religion always takes the form of a particular religion, The study of religion in school must therefore be the study of particular religions.

In traditional R.E. Christianity was the only religion studied (with the occasional exception of brief courses on other religions in the fifth or sixth form and the scandalously distorted picture of Judaism which was presented as part of the story of Christianity), but it is far from easy to understand what religion is by looking at only one religious tradition, especially if one is looking at it from the inside. It is by standing back that one is able to see a religion as a whole, with its manifold expression in the beliefs and way of life of individuals and societies. One of the most frequent comments made by young people who have taken part in the newer type of Religious Studies course in school, college or university is that through it they have gained a much clearer understanding of their own religion.

To many people the words 'understand' and 'study' imply purely intellectual activities, and the R.E. of the seventies has sometimes been criticised as too 'academic'. This, however, is to construe all these words in a very narrow way. It is also to forget that there are different kinds of understanding. Philip Phenix' analysis of the six ways in which man makes sense of his experience (pp.2–3) reminds us that each of the six is distinctive, each has its own characteristic structure and ideas. The way in which we develop competence in one realm, e.g., the arts, will be quite different from the way in which we develop it in others, e.g., the sciences, or personal relationships. Understanding in the synoptic realm cannot be achieved without a mastery of the very varied kinds of understanding required in the other realms of meaning. One of the most important of the other realms for religious education is the synnoetic realm—what it means to be a person in relation to other persons. This is certainly not an area in which much progress can be made by a purely intellectual study. The world of the emotions and of the imagination is of crucial importance here. The ability to enter imaginatively into another person's situation is essential for understanding what it would mean to take a religion seriously and this ability is developed in the early stages of schooling not by a direct study of religions but indirectly, particularly through the use of literature (see chapter 7). When children become absorbed in a story they identify with the characters in it, and through talking, writing, art, creative dance, etc., they enter into the story and become a part of it. From this 'inside' position they come to see situations and people in a new light. They are learning to 'feel' what it is like to be in another person's shoes.

What is required in religious education is some sort of balance. Traditional R.E. tended to put the emphasis on learning facts, the R.E. of the sixties swung to the other extreme with its almost exclusive emphasis on experience. The implicit and explicit elements should help us to maintain a balance, though these elements should not be thought of as making too sharp a division between emotion and intellect. There is a great deal of factual material involved in the implicit element, and it would be sad indeed if the explicit side of religious education was presented as merely a set of facts to be mastered by the pupils.

3

Order out of chaos

Discussion about religious education in recent years has centred largely on content and method, and far too little thought has been given to aims and objectives. One of the results is that the subject has lacked a logical structure.

In the traditional form of R.E. pupils might encounter some of the familiar stories from the Old Testament or from the life of Christ at any stage in their schooling from the reception class upwards. And there was no escape from the annual repetition of the Christmas and Easter stories.

After the first change in direction, in the sixties, the haphazardness of the traditional approach was replaced by an equally haphazard use of life-themes like 'Hands' or 'Journeys' or 'Light' in the early and middle years of schooling, and of discussions on topics like personal relationships and homelessness and advertising in the thirteen-plus years.

After the second change in direction, in the seventies, some teachers interpreted the more extensive use of world religions to mean that they had to present the religion of Hinduism or Islam to whatever age of children they taught, over-simplifying (and therefore distorting) it for younger pupils.

The chart on pp.140—1 is an attempt to show the different elements that make up religious education and the kind of sequence that is required for the pupils to build up an adequate understanding of religion by the time they leave secondary school.

It is important to stress that this chart is not intended to be a new kind of Agreed Syllabus. It would be wrong in any subject of the curriculum to suggest that teachers should merely take over a ready-made syllabus. Each school must work out how the aim of religious education can best be achieved in the light of its particular circumstances—whether it is in an isolated village or in the heart of an industrial city; whether it is multi-faith with Muslim, Hindu and Sikh pupils, multi-faith with Jewish and Greek and Turkish Cypriot pupils, multi-

13

cultural with West Indian pupils; whether it draws its pupils from homes where books and travel are taken for granted or is in an educational priority area; whether it has vertical grouping or team teaching or linked subjects or integrated studies—in fact all the variables that must be taken into consideration when planning a syllabus that will be right for that particular set of pupils.

Setting out a chart in this form can give a misleading impression of rigidity in another sense. The units are not meant to be in water-tight compartments, nor is it meant to suggest that only one type of scheme is possible. Festivals, for example, might be tackled as a study of the festivals of light which fall during the autumn term: the birthday of Guru Nanak in Sikhism, Divali in Hinduism, Chanukah (the Feast of Dedication) in Judaism and Christmas in Christianity. Alternatively, a class might undertake a fairly extensive exploration of the significance of the ways in which Christmas is observed, or again it might explore the underlying theme of festivals—man as a celebrating animal—and see the ways in which this is expressed in the great variety of celebrations to be found in society, from family anniversaries (e.g., birthdays) and local carnivals to Guy Fawkes Day and Remembrance Sunday, as well as the more obvious religious festivals.

Nor does the appearance of a unit on the chart mean that everything that falls under that title will be done when that particular unit is tackled. A secondary school with only five weeks available for a scheme on Judaism with its 13 year olds focussed on the Day of Atonement and the Passover. The lead-in from the Day of Atonement was prompted by the fact that the 1973 Arab-Israeli was war in progress—the war to which the citizen army of Israel had had to be called out from the synagogues during the 25 hour fast of the Day of Atonement. The scheme of work ended with the pupils participating in a carefully prepared and acted out Passover meal. This helped to convey not only information about the religion but also something of what it must feel like to be a member of a people for whom the Exodus events are part of their living experience and not just accounts of past history. The study of these two highly significant occasions in the Jewish year indicated to the 13 year olds the character of Judaism much more accurately and vividly than a more superficial treatment of a wider number of aspects of the religion could have done in the same number of weeks.

The chart makes a distinction between 'implicit' and 'explicit'

14

elements in religious education. The word 'implicit' is used where the significance for religion is implied but not directly referred to. It is concerned particularly with an exploration of, and reflection on, human experience. Religious education becomes 'explicit' when there is a direct study of something that is recognisably religious. There are some occasions when it is not possible to draw a sharp line between the implicit and the explicit elements, e.g., in the unit 'Creation Myths' (see p.152), but in the main the distinction is clear. The two elements may well be included in one unit, e.g., in 'What is Man?', 'Suffering' and 'Life after Death' (see pp.150–2), but what is important is that the teacher recognises the essential part which both elements play in the building up of an understanding of the nature of religion. (See chapters 4–7 for the implicit element.)

The arrangement of the chart in columns is designed to distinguish the different aspects of religious education. It does not mean that they must be kept separate in practice. The unit 'Home Life of Jewish Child at the Time of Jesus' might well be done along with either 'Homes and Families' or 'Growing Up'. There are numerous ways in which the material from different columns might be combined, depending on the particular interests of the class, topics which have just been tackled or are about to be done, etc.

The biblical and Christian material is shown separately to indicate how understanding in that field is gradually built up. But again it is not intended that it should always be taught separately. Units dealing with Christmas could be done within the unit 'Festivals' and the study of the Christian Scriptures belongs most naturally as part of the unit 'Sacred Writings'.

One of the criteria used for the placing of the units in relation to age groups is the stage of emotional and intellectual development of the pupils. Nine to eleven years is for most children the optimum stage at which to do 'Signs and Symbols', but this does not mean that they will then have 'done' signs and symbols. They are far too young to have any real understanding of the symbolic nature of religion, but the foundation will have been laid and it can be built on in later units, e.g., in a study of Coventry Cathedral, or in 'Festivals', 'Worship' and 'The Nature of Religious Language'. And if the pupils have done 'Sacred Places' before 'Signs and Symbols' they will be able to bring to the latter at least their knowledge of the picture symbols associated with the places of worship of different religions—the Jewish seven-branched candlestick, the Muslim crescent, the Christian cross, etc.

Teachers who have introduced schemes on worship in the secondary school will know the frustrating exercise it can be. Pupils assume that they know what worship is (haven't they been exposed to it daily from the age of five?) and they enter into heated debate about such issues as whether they approve of it, whether the language of worship is outdated, and whether worship should be expressed through the medium of teenage culture, and they miss altogether the real significance of worship. If a study of worship is to be really valuable it must come at a fairly mature stage of the pupils' development and it must be built on the foundations of earlier units. For example, if pupils have encountered such units as 'Sacred Places', 'Festivals', 'What is Belief?' and 'The Nature of Religious Language', they will have a store of understanding to bring to their exploration of what worship is (see chapter 15).

An essential prerequisite for understanding religion is knowing the ways in which it uses language, in contrast, for example, to the way in which the sciences use language. Most pupils (and many adults as well) assume that the language and methods which are proper in the empirical field—measurement, testing hypotheses by reference to sense experience, etc.—can be transferred to the realm of religion, with fatal consequences for their understanding of religion. The path suggested as leading up to the study of worship is one of the ways in which the distinctive uses of language in religion can be understood. Another path leads through 'Creation Myths', 'Signs and Symbols', 'Asking Questions' and 'What is Belief?' to 'The Nature of Religious Language' and perhaps on to an exploration of such philosophy of religion issues as miracles and the problem of evil.

There are two criteria which must always be met for teaching anything to anyone. One is the integrity of what is being taught (are we being true to the nature of the subject and not distorting it or trivialising it?), and the other is the interests, the abilities and the emotional and intellectual stage of development of those being taught. This suggested structure for religious education is an attempt to meet both these criteria.

It is also an attempt to give pupils at each stage of their schooling something which they can contribute to, and build in to, their study at the next and succeeding stages. Many teachers at secondary level experience a feeling of helplessness as they seek to make their religious education material come alive for their classes. On the one hand they are hampered because the pupils think they have heard it all before. They think they have met the religious questions—and in traditional R.E. they often have, though at a stage when they were too young to understand their nature and their significance—and they think they have met the 'answers'—which in traditional R.E. teachers often felt it their duty to give—and by about the age of twelve or thirteen most of them have rejected both the questions and the answers as irrelevant. On the other hand the teachers are faced by their pupils' ignorance of much that is needed for effective religious education at the secondary level. One cannot build a sound structure on inadequate foundations. It is essential to ask: What do pupils need to have understood if they are to make sense of a particular topic? and, What contribution are pupils able to bring to a topic from their earlier study? Only in this way is it possible to build up understanding.

One of the purposes of the structure suggested here is to create a sense of coherence in religious education. Units, especially for the younger children, might seem to be independent of each other but gradually the pupil should be able to recognise the relationship of the different elements and come to see the wholeness of what his religious education has given him.

The sparseness of some sections of the chart could give the misleading impression that teachers of small children can cheerfully ignore all the aspects of religious education apart from the human experience themes. The teacher must be aware of the kind of structure which is to be built if the foundations are to be the right ones. Systematic learning about the explicit elements of R.E. would be quite inappropriate, but a great deal of learning goes on at this stage in conversations with the teacher and with other children and in incidental discussions about topics which have arisen in the class. This may mean that the teacher contributes additional information or sets a child's comment in a wider context, but more often the teacher's contribution will take the form of questions. This assumes some understanding of the most appropriate questions to ask. It is important, for example, to know something about the Hindu festival of Divali if one is to encourage a Hindu child to share his experiences with others. And some of the traditional comments about Christmas can make it very difficult for either pupils or teachers to tackle this festival adequately in later years (see chapter 11).

Although no units apart from human experience themes are suggested for the under sevens the relevance of the different aspects for the younger age groups will be discussed within each of the chapters that follow.

Teachers of less able pupils, especially at secondary level, might also be tempted to feel that the approach to religious education outlined in this book does not meet their needs. It is therefore essential to stress that it is meant for all the ability groups which are to be found in the normal school system. The exposition in this book may sound intellectual— but then it is addressed to teachers and not to less able pupils.

Where the difference comes between R.E. for the less able and R.E. for the academic classes is not so much in the aims or even the topics but in the method of presentation and the length of time allowed. Less able pupils need to take things at a slower pace, to focus on fewer points and tackle them thoroughly. They need not only to start from the concrete and the observable (as pupils of all ages and abilities do) but their study needs to be firmly anchored there. Abstract issues have to be presented to them in the form of concrete examples. A general discussion on conflict of loyalties would be completely inappropriate but the use of a recognisable 'situation', in which a person is faced with a particular problem of conflict of loyalties, can produce lively and thoughtful discussion.

It is a fallacy to think that less academic pupils are not interested in serious topics. They probably have less experience and knowledge to help them to make rational judgments, they are unlikely to have sufficient command of language to express their thoughts and feelings with any competence, and they certainly won't be articulating ultimate questions in the sophisticated form in which they have been set down on pp.7—8. But this does not mean that they are never puzzled by life and by questions of meaning, and it may well be partly because they have not been encouraged to explore such questions in school that some of them cope with questions like 'Who am I?' and 'Is there any meaning in life?' by aggressive acts against a society which seems to them to deny their identity and their significance.

There are obviously units which would be inappropriate as they stand for less able pupils. 'The Nature of Religious Language' is an example. It would be ridiculous to tackle a unit which required the ability to think in philosophical categories. However, it would be wrong to tackle such a unit even with the most academic pupils if they had done no preparatory studies, and the sequence of units 'Signs and Symbols', 'Asking Questions' and 'What is Belief?' is a necessary one for all levels of ability. For the early leavers this sequence would have gone a considerable way to achieving its purpose (even though abler pupils would be able to take it further in their sixth form studies). In the process of helping the slow learners to think about the different ways in which we use words we are making a contribution in an area where it is most needed. Instead of neglecting schemes which involve language we should regard them as doubly important.

The question of teaching religious education to less able pupils is discussed further in Chapter 18, and one attempt to bring 'order out of chaos' for less academic classes in the secondary school is outlined there.

4

The implicit element in religious education

We shall start our description of the various elements in religious education by looking at the one which causes the greatest confusion—the approach from experience. In the R.E. of the sixties this came to be called 'implicit religion' because it made no explicit reference to religious topics. It is now more appropriately called the implicit element in religious education.

The distinction is important. 'Implicit religion' suggests that the pupils are growing in religious understanding without consciously realising it. Ronald Goldman's influential book was called, significantly, *Readiness for Religion*, and he stressed the need for an experiential approach in the 'pre-religious' stage of the child's development. In writing of intellectual, emotional and physical readiness for religion he defined religious education as the children's 'development towards confident relationships with their fellows and with God'. (*Readiness for Religion*, Routledge & Kegan Paul, 1965, p.57.) Writers on religious education frequently used the expression 'religious understanding', and no course for teachers was complete without its session on 'The development of children's religious concepts'. Expressions like 'hidden theology' and 'theology in non-theological language' (see the writer's article 'Life-themes—What are they?', *Learning for Living*, November, 1969) were used to demonstrate that doctrinal statements were really about such things as love and truth and justice and self-sacrifice and forgiveness, and that unless children had had experience of these qualities in their own lives the doctrines would remain largely meaningless.

Now all this is perfectly sound, but it assumes that the task of religious education is a confessional one—helping children to become religious. It still applies within a confessional context, such as the Church or the religious home, but it is no longer appropriate for religious education in the day school. We are concerned with the pupil's *understanding of religion* rather than his *religious understanding*.

20

What then is the justification for the implicit element in religious education?

We still put great emphasis on experience, both because children's experience plays an important part in their learning and in their development as persons, and because religions are concerned with man's experience.

Let us take the second reason first. Religions suggest answers to the ultimate questions which man asks. These questions are about the meaning of man's existence—his identity, his destiny, his relationship with others, his relationship with the natural world. Man has always asked such questions. For most of his history the 'why' and the 'how' questions were inextricably interwoven. He had no way of distinguishing between what was as yet unknown and what was in principle unknowable (in the empirical sense) and he gave the same kind of answers to the two different categories of question. Since the rise of modern science, however, man has gradually learnt to distinguish these questions. Many of man's 'how' questions have been answered and many more are on the way to being answered, but he is left with his 'why' questions. These are the kinds of questions to which there are no definitive answers in the human sciences. Answers to ultimate questions are never provable; they belong to the realm of belief and not to the realm of empirical knowledge.

To the question 'What is man?' a whole battery of scientists—anatomists, biochemists, neuro-physiologists, physicists, psychologists—will give us their answers, which we will readily accept. But when they have finished we are left with an irrepressible conviction that man is somehow more than the sum total of all those answers. There is something that eludes all that careful scientific analysis. What *is* man? Beliefs about the nature of man are a central part of all religions, and of non-religious systems as well.

The question 'What is man?' and the other ultimate questions—'Who am I?' 'Who is my neighbour?' 'Is there any meaning in life?' 'Is death the end?' 'How do I come to terms with suffering and evil?'—continue to haunt us. They do so because our life is constantly threatened by apparent meaninglessness. However much man achieves he is aware of the gulf that exists between his achievements and his aspirations. Even in the most highly developed technological societies he is at the mercy of forces which he cannot control. And even the most favoured individuals must be aware that, although their lives are well-ordered and comfortable, countless others have to endure the most appalling suffering and injustice.

There are three main areas in which man encounters that which is not at his disposal. First, it meets us in the form of the *situations* in which we have to act. Each situation is unpredictable. We may be certain that we have made watertight plans. And of course things may work out as we hoped they would. But equally some new factor may affect the situation, and upset our plans.

Secondly, it meets us in the form of *other people*. The people we encounter are independent, unpredictable realities in our lives. Like the situation, the person is 'given' to us in this way and in no other.

Thirdly, it meets us in the form of *the approaching future*, which is as unpredictable as our environment and the people we encounter. One of the inescapable elements in the future for each one of us is death. Man knows not only that he must die but that his life can be snuffed out at any moment.

Primitive man's fear of the unknown forces that controlled the thunderstorm or the drought or sickness may not be twentieth century man's fear, but he is still faced by the unknown and by the unpredictable.

A religion's answers to ultimate questions can be found in a systematic form in its doctrines or beliefs, but these are usually expressed in the kind of language that does not readily communicate the significance of the answer or its relation to one or more of the ultimate questions (especially to someone outside that particular religion). Non-Christians, for example, might well be forgiven for not realising that the Christian doctrine of the Incarnation—that God became man—includes the affirmation that at the heart of the universe lie personal values and not merely impersonal forces.

A study of the answers to ultimate questions given by the major religions and non-religious systems of belief should probably not be attempted much before the pupils are 13 or 14, but that study is unlikely to be effective unless the pupils have already thought about the kind of experience which gives rise to such questions.

In the following chapters we shall discuss different ways in which pupils can be encouraged to explore and reflect upon human experience, but first let us return to the other reason given for including an implicit element in religious education—the importance of the child's own experience.

The implicit element in religious education

Religious education has no monopoly of concern for the personal development of the child. This is the shared concern of the whole school, but religious and non-religious systems of belief all involve the conviction, in whatever way they express it, that human flourishing matters, and it would be strange indeed if we were content to teach our pupils about this and yet care nothing for *their* flourishing. This is important all the way through school but it is doubly important in the early years. No teacher of young children needs to be told how crucial to the child's later development and to his ability to establish positive personal relationships are the experiences he has in early childhood, particularly in relation to adults.

Equally, no teacher of young children needs to be told how important experience is in the learning process. This has been amply demonstrated in maths. And in English children who are going to write about the wind no longer merely sit in the classroom and talk about it; they first go out on to the playground and feel it. And talking about being kind to animals is no substitute for caring for pets; real learning can take place when the children discover how dependent the animals are on them for food and cleanliness and a sense of security. A negative example was provided by a class of six year olds, observed in the middle of the theme 'People who help us'. The walls were resplendent with pictures and writing about people in the community but the atmosphere in the classroom was, unusually for this age, competitive in the extreme, with children determinedly refusing to share scissors and paint and glue. On the more positive side the class of ten year olds who made Christmas gifts and delivered them personally to elderly people living alone gained more in understanding than they would have gained from merely talking about the importance of giving at Christmas time.

Experience is important in another respect too. Children interpret in the context of their experience, and many words and phrases which adults regard as simple and straightforward can convey quite a different meaning to children. This is particularly true in religious education. Ronald Goldman tells the story of a young child who heard the parable of the Prodigal Son (*Readiness for Religion*, p.44). At the end of it he said, 'I do think his Daddy might have gone with him!' Goldman comments, 'The distortion is complete, for instead of hearing the story of a loving father, he has heard the story of a neglectful one.' What small child from a caring home is left to go out into a situation of danger by himself while his father merely stands at the gate waiting for him to come back?

We all have a fund of stories of children's misunderstandings in the field of religion—from 'Harold be thy name' to 'Pontius the Pilot'—and yet it is surprising how long it has taken us to see these not only as amusing stories but as pointers to the kind of distortion that is likely to occur when we try to teach children things that are too difficult for their stage of experience and understanding.

With the explicit elements in religious education being so complex, the implicit element is the absolutely essential foundation, and for the under sevens it is really the only aspect that is appropriate in a non-confessional situation.

It is perhaps necessary to make the point—very strongly—that this is *not* the same thing as saying that one need not bother with religious education for the early years of schooling. The implicit element is very much part of religious education and unless it has been tackled effectively the teachers of the older age groups are going to find it difficult if not impossible to deal adequately with the subject in its more recognisable form.

If one is to attempt to understand religion, and particularly to understand a way of looking at the world different from one's own, then one must have an enquiring mind, one must feel secure enough to be prepared to venture into new realms, one must be able to accept differences without feeling threatened, one must have the confidence to be able to accord positive value to other people's beliefs without necessarily losing one's own. It is the foundation of these qualities that is laid in the early years of childhood.

5

Human experience themes

The rather clumsy expression 'human experience themes' has been used in order to distinguish this kind of theme from the 'themes' or 'life-themes' of the R.E. of the sixties. The term 'life-theme' was coined by Ronald Goldman who described them (*Readiness for Religion*, p.110) as 'teaching by means of themes based upon the real life experiences of the children . . . Life-themes relate religion to life by emphasising the total unity of experience'.

The pattern established at that time was followed with little variation for several years. It was very like the familiar primary school topic but with biblical material added. As it turned out the effect was the opposite of what Goldman had intended. Instead of emphasising the total unity of experience, life-themes appeared to separate religion and life. The religious element was widely identified with the biblical material and life-themes appeared to be mainly about 'life' with 'religion' brought in occasionally. The uneasiness of many teachers was expressed by one who complained that if a child sneezed and was away from school for a day he could miss his religious education for the term.

Most of the life-themes, or themes as they soon came to be called, were about such things as 'Hands' and 'Fire' and 'Journeys', and they moved from the exploration of the children's experience to stories about Jesus' hands, or methods of cooking in Palestine and fire from heaven in the Elijah story, or the journeys of Moses and the Israelites in the wilderness, the flight into Egypt and Paul's missionary journeys. However, the original *Readiness for Religion* series also included such things as 'Light' and 'Bread' and 'Sheep and Shepherds', where the move to the biblical material was not just inspired by a superficial verbal association. The Palestinian experience of shepherd life was an important element in understanding the biblical image of the Good Shepherd. There is real justification in religious education for exploring the way of life that produced the great biblical images, but this is most appropriately done as a study of life in Bible times (see pp.92—3) and should not be confused with the exploration of the children's experience.

The human experience themes in column one of the chart on pp.140--1 are only examples of the kind of theme which makes a positive contribution to the pupil's religious education. Other themes may well be added, particularly in the First school years.

How do we decide which themes are suitable, and how should they be developed once we have chosen them?

The purpose of themes is to encourage the pupils to explore and reflect upon human experience, at that stage in their development when each theme is most significant for them. This gives us a clue to the timing of the themes. 'Homes and Families' is best done with the 5—7 year olds because that is the time when their lives are centred on their homes and families. One of the new Agreed Syllabuses suggested this theme for the Middle school years. Of course it can be done then, but 11—13 year olds particularly are noticeably less enthusiastic about their families than 5—7 year olds, and will respond less eagerly to a series of lessons which focus on the values of living together in families just at the stage when the young adolescent is developing feelings of independence in relation to his family.

By the same reasoning 'Fear' belongs at about the 13 year old stage. This is not to suggest that younger children have no fears. They certainly do, but these are best dealt with in other ways—incidentally, or by adults giving a sense of security, or by the use of suitable stories, or by creative drama and writing. The more systematic exploration is most helpful at that stage in adolescence when fears of all kinds develop, and the youngster feels that he is alone in being afraid.

'Hands' is suggested for the 5—7 year olds because this is the great period of development in the control of the hands—learning to button coats, tie knots, write, paint, etc. And with what a sense of triumph is each new task mastered! In the next two or three years the child makes equally marked progress in the control of his feet. It is the age of skipping, hop-scotch, football, etc., so this is a good time for a theme on 'Feet'.

'Courage' is appropriate for the 9—11 year olds because this is when they reach the peak of their admiration for brave deeds, though it is courage shown in practical ways that makes the greatest appeal at this age. Subtler forms of courage can be appreciated more easily by older pupils and will emerge in the themes suggested for adolescents—'Barriers', 'Fear', 'Conflict'.

Matching the theme to the emotional development of the pupils is thus one important factor in selecting human experience themes. And it helps to avoid that haphazardness which characterised the R.E. of the sixties.

Another factor is the way in which the children are gradually building up their understanding of human experience. Sequence matters here.

One group of related themes is 'Colours' (5—7), 'Night and Day' (7—9) and 'Sight' (9—11). This sequence is directed mainly at encouraging the child to explore the beauty and the order and the complexity of the natural world. This is certainly not intended to be a sentimental approach to nature. Nature's ruthlessness is part of its complexity, and the pupil who learns about the phenomenal eyesight of the bird of prey cannot avoid encountering the problem of the hunted as well as the hunter. However, the emphasis in this group of themes is not on the dark side of life. The purpose is rather to increase the pupils' awareness that man is part of the natural world, that he is dependent on it and that he has responsibility to it. (See pp.42 f. for discussion of the dark side of life.)

Another group of related themes is 'Homes and Families' and 'Babies' (5—7), 'Growing Up' (7—9), 'Who am I?' (9—11), 'What is Man?' (13—15). This sequence offers a steady expansion, appropriate to each stage of the pupil's development, of the understanding of what it is to be human. This does not mean a mere repetition at different stages but it does mean that what the pupil has gained at one stage is taken up and used to deepen and entend his understanding at the next stage.

'What is Man?' is a unit of study requiring careful consideration of the questions raised about man by the human sciences and of the answers suggested by the major religions and non-religious systems of belief. It will be a much profounder and more worthwhile enterprise if the pupils are able to bring to it all that is involved in the earlier themes in the group—belonging, caring, sharing, growing, the miracle of learning to walk and talk, the wonder of the human body and of the human personality, the mystery of change and yet continuity as we grow up, hopes and fears, self-sacrifice and selfishness, the ability to create and the ability to destroy. What *is* man? The First and Middle school themes are not designed to 'give answers', but rather to raise questions and to open children's eyes to the wonder and the complexity of life.

We can summarise our criteria for regarding a theme as making a contribution to religious education in this way: Does it help the pupil to understand himself, other people and the natural world better? Does it help him to understand better his own relationship to other people and to the natural world? Does it raise questions about man's experience and about the mystery of what it is to be human?

If we follow these guide-lines then there is likely to be some coherence in our choice of human experience themes. Otherwise, as John Hull pointed out in 1970 ('The Theology of Themes', Albert Leavesley Memorial Lecture, Churches of Christ, Christian Education Committee), a theme can 'go wild'. He wrote, 'Although with wise and disciplined use thematic teaching can be excellent, there is some evidence that the method is running to seed. A recent textbook contains details of a theme called 'All work and no play' which consists of thirty-two topics, ranging from the advantages of midweek travel, through places Jesus visited, to holidays in space, and including how to avoid travel sickness, words which have entered the English language from other languages, a map of Palestine two thousand years ago, how people ceberate Christmas, the earth's atmosphere, the Egyptian myth of the creation of the world, Darwinian evolution, horoscopes, bank holidays and how to make an electric map of Palestine complete with wiring diagram.' This was perhaps an extreme example but many of the themes published in the late sixties and early seventies exhibited a similar magpie-like tendency to bring together a conglomeration of ideas only vaguely related to the central theme.

This is not to suggest that the implicit element in religious education is catered for only in a human experience theme. A general primary school topic can also make a valuable contribution. To argue for a strictly disciplined theme is a plea for clear thinking, not a criticism of the general topic which may branch out in a number of different directions (though no less than the human experience theme does it demand clear thinking and carefully thought out aims).

General topics, for example the Farm, the Post Office, the Neighbourhood, Water, Space, are extending the pupils' understanding of the world, but the criteria set out above are met more specifically in certain aspects of the topic, for example, if, in finding out about the work of the local postman, the children are encouraged to see it from his point of view—what time does he have to get up in the morning? how far does he have to travel to work and how does he get there? what does he feel about setting out at that hour in winter or in rainy weather? how heavy is the bag he has to carry when he starts his round? what are some of the problems he encounters on his round? what disadvantages does he find in the hours he has to keep? This approach helps the children to gain a sympathetic understanding of what it would be like to be a post-man, and not merely a detached knowledge of what he does.

Similarly, in a topic on the neighbourhood the application of the criteria for the implicit element in religious education will mean that the children's attention is directed not only to external features—layout, architecture, facilities, etc.—but also to human values—the advantages and disadvantages for mothers of young children, the problems the local shop-keeper has to face in competition with the supermarkets in the nearest main shopping area, the effects of a proposed new road or housing development. Conflict of interest is probably the most common feature of life in a community. Seldom do the decisions we make benefit everyone involved, whether at the level of the family or the local community or at national or international level. It would be wrong to protect children from this form of reality by suggesting that decisions were clear-cut and straightforward and could be described simply as 'good' or 'bad'. By helping them to see the advantages and disadvantages on both sides in, for example, the use of open fields or land with trees on it for a housing estate, or the destruction of houses for a by-pass to divert traffic from a congested area, we are increasing their awareness of the kind of human experience which leads man to ask at least one of the ultimate questions—'Who is my neighbour?'

Traditionally in religious education the question 'Who is my neigh-bour?' has been answered by the parable of the Good Samaritan. Now this parable is one of the most profound stories in the New Testament. It extends the concept of neighbour from a member of one's own group or nation (the 'kith and kin' principle) to anyone in need. It breaks down all barriers of exclusiveness. The teaching of this parable provides Christians with the framework within which they have to make decisions which involve conflict of interest: the principle that I do not have a greater obligation to 'my' group just because it *is* 'my' group. It does not answer the question 'Who is my neighbour?' in specific conflict of interest situations.

It is not suggested that teachers should try to provide answers to the conflict of interest problems which their pupils encounter, and to try to reach a class decision, for example by a vote, is an arid exercise indeed. It implies that decisions on complex matters can be made without knowledge of all the factors—economic, political and social—that are involved, and it encourages the pupils to form the kind of prejudiced judgment which is so often a feature of adult debates about local and national issues. Individual pupils may well have their own convictions about which would be the right course of action, and in their discussions and their writing they will work out their reasons for these convictions. This is highly desirable but it is very different from suggesting that there is one 'right' solution to the problem.

The above examples have been taken from the type of work suitable for 7—11 year olds. The same principles apply in integrated studies with older pupils, but such studies also raise wider issues and these are dealt with in a separate section (see chapter 17).

To move to the younger age group—5—7—it is perhaps important to emphasise that, although the criteria for the implicit element in religious education apply here, the suggested list of human experience themes does not mean that formal schemes of work are being advocated. It would be quite wrong just to work through a ready-made theme. A chance incident will be the most frequent stimulus for a theme; for example, the children's fascination with a rainbow may lead into an exploration of colours, a child's announcement that he is going to have a baby brother or sister may lead into a theme on babies, class experiments with cooking may lead into the idea of having a party and so develop into thinking about parties in general.

Lists of themes for this age group often suggest such things as 'Friends', 'Presents', 'Giving,' 'Helping'. It *may* be right for a particular class to develop one or more of these themes, but normally they lend themselves either to incidental treatment when the topic arises, or to inclusion within other themes, for example, 'Giving' belongs within 'Parties', 'Helping' within 'Homes and Families' and 'Babies', 'Presents' will be included in 'Parties' but it will also come up in connection with Christmas. One of the marks of the good teacher is the ability to pick up and use profitably ideas as they arise, and to discriminate between the idea which should be discussed briefly and the one which it would be right to develop with that particular group of children.

Stories from the Bible have little or nothing to contribute to human experience themes with the younger children, but have they any place in later years? In our reaction against the inevitable dragging in of biblical material which has characterised theme teaching we must be careful not to exclude it as unthinkingly as it used to be included. A theme is certainly not made religious by the addition of biblical material. It is not even made more religious. Human experience themes stand in their own right as an important element in religious education. But we no more want to forbid the use of the Bible as a source of illustrative material than we want to forbid the use of any other source. We shall ask of any illustration we consider using: Does it help the pupils to understand more deeply the kind of experience with which the theme is dealing?

The story of David and Jonathan (1 Samuel 20) is a good story of a boy's courage, and 9—11 year olds are capable of grasping the circumstances surrounding the incident—without which Jonathan's courage would scarcely have any meaning. On the other hand, the story of David and Goliath (1 Samuel 17), useful as it may be in other contexts, is not nearly such a good illustration of courage. It does not require a very perceptive nine year old to realise that David, who as a shepherd would be expert in the use of a sling, would know that he could strike Goliath with a stone long before he came within range of Goliath's spear or dagger.

Compilers of themes on 'Feet' frequently suggest the use of the story of Jesus washing the disciples' feet. This is a clear example of the artificial use of biblical material which results from merely verbal association. This Gospel story is about humility and service, and the reference to feet is purely incidental. It no more increases children's awareness of feet and what they can do than the story of Samuel anointing David as king by pouring oil on his head extends their understanding of heads. Biblical material would be completely inappropriate in a theme on 'Feet'.

On the other hand, 'Growing Up' lends itself to thinking about the similarities and differences in growing up in different parts of the world or in different ages, and what it would be like to grow up in Palestine at the time of Jesus is just as good a candidate for inclusion as growing up in ancient Egypt or growing up in the land of the Eskimos. And although on the chart the unit 'Home Life of Jewish Child at the Time of Jesus' is in a different column that does not mean that it must be kept separate. A teacher may well want to introduce it at the same time as, or soon after, 'Growing Up'.

With older pupils who have already developed an antipathy towards the Bible we shall have to be very cautious about the use of biblical material in themes, but where pupils have had a less traditional kind of religious education at the primary stage it should be much easier to use biblical illustrations. However, this will seldom mean, for example in the theme on 'Fear', suddenly presenting the class with a Bible story about someone who was afraid or who conquered fear. Of much more positive value is the illustration produced by the pupils from something they have studied earlier, perhaps the unit on Masada, or one of the biblical image themes. This is why the teacher has to see religious education as a whole and has to keep in mind what contribution he wants the pupils to be able to bring to each successive unit.

Finally, how seriously do we take the frequently repeated maxim, 'start with the pupils' own experience'? With the youngest age groups it is obviously right, but we have to ask whether it is such sound advice with older pupils. Middle school pupils are perfectly capable of going straight into a study of the Vikings or the Incas, and they can equally go straight into a study of life in Palestine, or the structure of the eye. Cross references to their own experience will be made naturally during their study; they don't need to begin that way. During this outward-looking period of a child's development, when his curiosity is at its height, an undue emphasis on his own experience may seem slightly precious.

For adolescent pupils there is an added reason for not starting with their own experience. This is a highly self-conscious age, the approval of the peer group matters tremendously, and there is great reluctance to reveal what one really thinks. That is why the theme on 'Fear' suggests starting with the kinds of fear that children experience, then moving on to the fears of other sections of the community. In this way the pupils may feel able to express their own fears, in the guise of other people's, and as the theme progresses and they discover that their own fears are not unique they may well gain the confidence to share them more openly.

But at each age we must beware of the danger of appearing to moralise. Adolescents are particularly sensitive to what they describe as 'being got at'. The purpose of human experience themes is to enable our pupils to explore and reflect on human experience, with all its variety, its complexity, its mystery; it is not to enable to us to mould our pupils into a particular pattern or to suggest that there is one right way (the teacher's?) to think and to act.

6

Biographies

Biographical material has had a place in religious education for many decades, and there are very good reasons for retaining it today. However, this does not mean that we should necessarily use the same material or that our aims remain the same.

As long as it was believed that the purpose of R.E. was to lead pupils to see the truth and value of Christianity, it was natural to show the influence of this faith in the lives of Christian men and women. Now that our aim is to help pupils not only to understand what religion is but also what it would mean to take a religion seriously, we shall need to extend our list beyond the ranks of Christians, and include men and women whose lives and work are clearly motivated by the beliefs (religious or non-religious) they hold. Examples of this kind of person are Mario Borrelli, Mother Teresa and Toyohiko Kagawa.

When biographical material is used for this purpose (and it should be so used only with older pupils) we shall not include stories just because the hero happened to exhibit qualities of courage or compassion or self-sacrifice. It is true that everyone's actions are influenced by what he believes, but we can demonstrate the relationship between faith and life most clearly if we restrict ourselves to examples in which the relationship is explicit and the beliefs are the acknowledged driving force of the person's life.

But there is another purpose for which we may use biographical material, and that is in relation to the implicit element in R.E.—helping pupils to explore the nature of human experience. Now our list of possible candidates for inclusion is much more extensive. Religious beliefs will be important in the lives of some of these people, in others they will play a minor part or be non-existent, but what matters here is the human qualities they show and the extent to which a study of them stirs the imagination and gives a greater insight into the depth and variety of such qualities. Social reformers, such as Danilo Dolci, are appropriate here, and men like Captain Oates with his selfless act of courage in Antarctica, but so also is the young Jewish girl, Anne Frank, in hiding from the Nazis, and Helen Keller, who overcame such over-whelming handicaps, and Beethoven, who wrote his Ninth Symphony after he had become completely deaf.

In the previous chapter we discussed the importance of selecting themes according to the pupils' stage of development. This is equally important in the field of biographies. The compilers of the older Agreed Syllabuses scattered the names of 'Friends and Followers of Jesus' across their pages with a cheerful lack of regard for their suitability for the age of the pupils. David Livingstone, Mary Slessor, Albert Schweitzer, St. Francis, St. Patrick, Elizabeth Fry and others cropped up in one syllabus or another for every age group from infant to senior secondary!

There are two main criteria to be applied when choosing biographical material. First, do the qualities which the subject of the biography shows make an appeal to the pupils at that particular stage in their development?

Nine to eleven year olds, for example, are at a very practical stage. They enjoy the story of James Evans who worked among the Cree Indians of Canada. Before translating the Bible into Cree Evans had to reduce the language to writing. Then he melted down the lead linings of tea chests to make type for printing and he treated the bark of birch trees to make 'paper'. In addition, the syllabic alphabet which Evans invented makes an immediate appeal to an age group that adores working out codes.

Children of this age also admire personal courage and acts of bravery and they can therefore enter enthusiastically into the stories of the lives of men like Theodore Pennell who, in the early part of this century, went unarmed among the fierce warrior tribes of Afghanistan, or Fr. Damien, who went to live on the leper island of Molokai at a time when leprosy was incurable and who caught the dreaded disease himself. On the other hand, the personal courage of Toyohiko Kagawa of Japan is not nearly so likely to capture the imagination of this age group. Kagawa suffered from bad health throughout his life becuase as a young man he went to live in the slums and shared the appalling conditions of squalor there with those he had come to help. Adolescents can appreciate such acts of identification with the outcasts of society, but 9—11 year olds, with their practical bias and their tendency to see things in black and white terms, are more likely to be critical. They will probably say that if Kagawa had not moved into the slums his health might not have suffered and he could have accomplished even more than he did. Equally, Kagawa's unwavering pacifism, in his own personal encounters with violence as well as in relation to his country's war efforts, does not make a strong appeal to children who have been learning to stand up for themselves against bullying and whose sense of justice is satisfied only when the villain gets as good as he gives.

In the same way the philosophies of non-violence of men like Mahatma Gandhi and Martin Luther King are more easily understood by older pupils than by younger ones.

The second criterion to be applied is whether the background and experience of the pupils are sufficient to enable them to appreciate the qualities of the person being studied. To appreciate adequately the achievements of the social reformers, it is essential to be able to visualise the social conditions of the time. Elizabeth Fry's heroic work among the women prisoners of her day will be reduced to the proportions of the activities of a lady bountiful if the children are not aware of the horrors of the women's prisons and the level of bestiality to which the inmates had been driven—and which of us would want primary school children to know what it is like in women's prisons today, let alone the unspeakable conditions of Elizabeth Fry's day?

For this reason as well as for the reason outlined above, the story of Kagawa is suitable for adolescents rather than for younger pupils. Much of his work was in industrial relations and he fought for the establishment of trade unions, but this will mean little until the pupils are old enough to understand the conditions of poverty and powerlessness under which millions of Japanese workers struggled to survive in the twenties and thirties. Similarly the work of Martin Luther King can be understood only in the context of the relationships between the races in the U.S.A., and this involves the ability to grasp the historical background as well as the contemporary situation.

To attempt this at too early an age is to invite an oversimplifying of the issues, with a consequent division into 'goodies' and 'baddies'. If we find that we are having to treat highly complex questions on a superficial level in order to present them to our pupils then we are definitely trying to introduce the material too soon. We should be asking not, 'What is the earliest age at which the pupils can understand this character?' but 'What is the best age?' As with all other aspects of the subject we should be aiming to get the maximum value from our lessons, and for that the timing is crucial.

A slightly different kind of problem is raised by the story of Albert Schweitzer. Primary school children are quite capable of recognising the courage and dedication which sent Schweitzer to a remote part of the African continent to labour through half a century providing medical help for the people in the area around Lambarene, but there was much more to Schweitzer's life than this, and it is the 'much more' in any biography that gives the story its distinctive flavour and prevents it from becoming just one more account of a missionary doctor in a foreign land. It is only senior pupils already thinking seriously about their own careers who can really appreciate the significance of Schweitzer's sacrificing of a brilliant academic career, or of his gaining of doctorates in four completely different disciplines, or of his renown as an interpreter of Bach, or of the publication of his book *The Quest of the Historical Jesus* which marked a turning-point in New Testament studies.

Even more difficult for younger pupils is Schweitzer's paternalistic attitude to the Africans to whom he devoted his life. (How honest is it to teach about Schweitzer and ignore what was an integral part of his story?) Senior pupils, however, can understand that Schweitzer's paternalism was characteristic of the nineteenth century society in which he grew up, that he was a child of his age as we all are of ours, and that this does not prevent us from marvelling at his achievements.

A different problem again is raised by the story of Gladys Aylward. This is often suggested as suitable for young children because it includes the account of her long trek across the mountains with nearly a hundred children. No one could fail to be filled with admiration for the indomitable courage of this amazing woman but how do we present the deliverance from crises which came as a direct answer to prayer? This aspect is sensitively handled in Alan Burgess' full length biography *The Small Woman*, but in shorter versions for children it is usually stated much more crudely. To children such 'answers to prayer' can only appear as concrete examples of God's intervention in the world, and they are likely to be left with the impression that this power can somehow or other be 'turned on'. Sooner or later they are going to realise that not only does God not answer their prayers for help in the consistent way in which he apparently answered Gladys Aylward's prayers, but that there are many other saintly Christians who have suffered tragically and who have not been delivered from dangers. In adolescence this can be a valuable subject for discussion, and it can lead on to a consideration of the different ways in which Christians understand the power and the purpose of prayer, but most children at the earlier concrete stage of intellectual development are not yet mature enough for such a discussion. Gladys Aylward's belief in the power of prayer must be seen in the context of a total relationship of faith; viewed in isolation from that context, it is more likely to appear to children to involve a mechanical response to a request for help.

If biographies are worth including in religious education they are worth doing properly. There is little to be gained from just reading to the pupils the kind of simplified, summarised story so often produced for use in schools. The teacher must know the material very well and, particularly with the Middle school age group, be able to tell at least part of the story in dramatic narrative form. The pupils must have access to good reference books—history, geography, encyclopedias, etc.— for writing and illustrative work and, where it is available, to primary sources, e.g., letters, extracts from diaries, etc.

The aim of using biographical material will not have been accomplished if the pupils do not feel that they really 'know' the person they have studied and if they have not been able to enter into his situation. This means a great deal of work on the pupils' part, probably best done in groups, and culminating in something tangible (or audible, such as a tape-recording). For instance, a class working on the story of Mario Borrelli might prepare and tape a series of interviews—with a hotel proprietor in Naples, with a British tourist, with one of the scugnizzi, with Borrelli himself, and with the aged cardinal who gave Borrelli permission to become a scugnizzo.

Pupils will obviously gain a great deal more if they read during their school years a smaller number of biographies and do them thoroughly than if they learn about a larger number of people more superficially. It is also better for the hard-pressed teacher to master a limited number of biographies. This points up, however, the need for consultation between teachers, especially in Junior and Middle schools. It would be unfortunate if a set of pupils found that the only biographies they ever did were social reformers, or missionaries, and they missed the opportunity of exploring a wider range of human experiences and achievements.

There are a number of pitfalls lying in wait for the teacher who ventures into biographical studies. In the first place, there is the temptation, by no means always avoided by the writers to whom the teacher has to turn, to make the story more dramatic by presenting the person as larger than life. It is no help to the pupil, especially at the adolescent stage, to be left with the impression that the subject of the biography had no faults. It is both true to life, and of some encouragement to lesser mortals, that acts of personal bravery and self-sacrifice, and great achievements in science or the arts or social reform can be accomplished by men and women who are less than perfect.

Secondly, there is a danger of conflict of aims. This is especially acute in stories of the lives of European missionaries or others whose field of service has been in what we now call the Third World. Teachers who care passionately about race relations might easily find themselves reinforcing racial prejudice by presenting stories of the courageous white man who faced untold dangers from hostile natives to preach the Gospel in a 'heathen' land. Many of these men and women, especially in the nineteenth century, worked among primitive tribal peoples, and a description of their work, accurate as it might be, could easily leave the pupils with the idea, for example, that all Africans are illiterate and live in small huts in jungle clearings. Biographical material of this kind has therefore to be handled very carefully and almost certainly not in isolation.

The story of a European working in a particular country might be linked with the story of a national of that country whose achievements have been equally noteworthy. Alternatively, the story of a European working in primitive conditions can be seen in perspective when it is only one element in a study of a particular region, and when the pupils are also learning that today the country has large cosmopolitan cities, a complex and sophisticated economy, schools, hospitals and centres of higher education, that it has its own artists and writers, and that it is governed by its own nationals.

A similar problem has arisen because of the wholly admirable desire of teachers to make their pupils aware of the hunger and the homelessness of so much of the world's population, and to stimulate both the imagination and the desire to help. The danger comes from the fact that the areas of greatest need happen to be the areas where the greatest number of black and brown-skinned peoples live, and the cumulative effect of the emphasis over several years of schooling on the needs of the Third

World may well create the impression of the successful and prosperous light-skinned races doling out charity to the unfortunate dark-skinned ones. Again, steps have to be taken to counteract this impression, partly by looking at situations of need among white people, and partly by focussing attention on the contribution being made, e.g., in national and international projects such as those of the U.N. agencies, by men of all colours.

We have been considering mainly people of the last two or three centuries, but R.E. syllabuses have traditionally included stories of the saints, at least in their primary sections. Here we meet another problem which comes under the heading of 'conflict of aims'. Part of our purpose as teachers is to help children, especially at the Junior school stage, to sort out fact from fantasy, and yet the stories of almost all the saints include legendary material.

We can turn this problem to our advantage by using such stories to help the children to understand how legendary material gathers round certain people, and how it tells us something important about the person even if it isn't literally true. Because we have so little real bio-graphical material about most of the saints, we shall seldom be using their stories for the purposes for which we include biographies in religious education, and we shall certainly have to restrict our use of such stories to the age group which can appreciate the growth of legendary material.

Teachers of younger children will have seen all the familiar characters diappearing from their section of the syllabus, for at the First school stage there is little place for biographies.

In school, where our task is neither to teach for belief nor to initiate children into any one religious tradition, the first reason for the use of biographies—to show the relationship between belief and life—is inappropriate. The children are too young to understand what a belief system is, let alone to consider alternative belief systems. (In a confess-ional context the situation is different. For children who are growing up within a religious faith only one set of beliefs is involved, and some of these may well be demonstrated through stories of people who profess that faith.)

The other main purpose of biographies—enabling pupils to explore and reflect upon human experience—is likely to be more effectively met by the use of children's literature. Good stories which have been written especially for children are better than simplified accounts of the lives of people whose actions are set in the adult world and whose achievements will appear simplistic or distorted if they are reduced to the level of understanding and experience of the under nines. Fortunately there is plenty of good literature, and we turn to that now.

7

The use of literature

Literature, used here as an umbrella word for three different kinds of writing—fiction, myths and legends—can make a significant contribution to the implicit element in religious education, and it is a particularly important ingredient of human experience themes.

In contrast to the shortage of really good resource books for the explicit side of religious education there is a wealth of high quality literature for children and young people. Most teachers will have their own preferences, and the ideal policy is for each teacher to build up his own collection, but on pp.192—6 there are some suggestions for those who are just embarking on teaching or who have not previously thought about which stories might be particularly useful in religious education. The age ranges given are intended to be only a very general guide; in certain circumstances a story might be used for a much wider age range. Only the teacher can know whether a story would be right for a given class.

Sometimes it will be best just to read a book, or extracts from a book, to the class, and pupils should certainly be introduced to books for individual reading, but some stories lend themselves to considerable follow-up work by the pupils—creative writing (including the writing of poetry), frieze-making, etc. However, whenever a story is being shared in class the pupils should be encouraged to talk about it. For small children this could provide a very necessary opportunity to share similar experiences in their own lives, or it could enable them to bring to the surface and express anxieties which would otherwise remain hidden, for example, sadness at the death of a family pet, as in *The Tenth Good Thing about Barney* by Judith Viorst, or the feeling of being displaced by the new baby in the family, as in *Peter's Chair* by Ezra Jack Keats.

Coming to terms with the dark side of life is one of the most difficult but one of the most essential aspects of growing up. Fortunately many of the stories for children are ideal for this purpose. There are stories in which children face fears and disappointments (e.g., *A Dog so Small* by Philippa Pearce, *The Boy who was Afraid* by Armstrong Sperry), stories in which they experience failure and loneliness and rejection (e.g., *The Secret Garden* by Frances Hodgson Burnett, *The Children of the House* by Philippa Pearce and Brian Fairfax-Lucy), stories in which the death of someone close to them seems to make life meaningless (e.g., *Pauline* by Margaret Storey, *Pennington's Seventeenth Summer* by K. M. Peyton), and as our pupils find their own emotions and sometimes even their own situations reflected in the stories they are able to identify with the characters and explore not only the experiences but the ways in which the characters faced up to those experiences and lived through them. The element of realism in contemporary writing is to be welcomed. Stark and utter tragedy is avoided, for in the world of children there is, and must always be, hope, but on the other hand all the difficulties do not suddenly disappear as if someone had waved a magic wand. Problems are resolved, sometimes by courage and self-sacrifice, sometimes through friendship and acceptance by others, sometimes through acceptance of self, sometimes through seeing situations—and people—in a new light, but this does not mean that everyone therefore 'lives happily ever after'. John Rowe Townsend's books *Gumble's Yard* and *The Intruder*, are particularly good for this recognition that life must go on, and that what has been changed by the end of the story is not so much the situation as the person himself.

To understand oneself is a necessary part of growing up and stories which describe an adolescent's search for identity, with its aspirations and its fears, its humiliations and its achievements, can make a powerful contribution to our pupils' development as persons. Good examples of such books are *Warrior Scarlet* by Rosemary Sutcliff and *One is One* by Barbara Leonie Picard. Also valuable are the stories of courage, not just the courage of an act of bravery in the heat of a battle or some other crisis, but the courage which makes possible the enduring of suffering and hardship over a long period, as depicted, for example, in the life of a pioneering family in America in the nineteenth century (*The Little House on the Prairie* by Laura Ingalls Wilder), or the Polish Jewish family deported to Siberia during the second world war (*The Endless Steppe* by Esther Hautzig).

The experience of not being understood by adults or by the peer group is particularly acute in early adolescence, and this is captured in a number of stories (e.g., *Charley* by Joan G. Robinson, *Josh* by Ivan Southall) which serve to reassure the reader that his particular problem is a familiar part of human experience and not, as it often seems, proof of overwhelming inadequacy. They also serve to increase awareness of what others may be feeling. Stories about someone who is treated as an outcast by the group (e.g., *The Diddakoi* by Rumer Godden, *The Witch's Brat* by Rosemary Sutcliff) can heighten pupils' sensitivity towards those to whom otherwise they might be unthinkingly cruel.

The temptation to judge others only by what we see on the surface is strong in children and young people (it is not always resisted by adults) but the detail into which a book can go makes it possible to penetrate the hidden depths and discover perhaps the frustration and the mental conflict which take place before certain words are spoken or actions undertaken, and the feeling of utter helplessness afterwards that the words cannot be unsaid or the actions undone. What is revealed is the pressures on people which cause them to react as they do. A powerful book which comes into this category is *The Stronghold* by Mollie Hunter. To understand what motivates a person is to have made great progress in the ability to stand in other people's shoes, and without this ability no real understanding of religion is possible.

The questions which young people are having to sort out for themsevles can sometimes be more easily recognised if they are distanced. They may be distanced merely by being seen in someone else's life, but they are sometimes more effectively distanced by being seen in a completely different context. In *Stig of the Dump* by Clive King, Barney sees familiar things through the eyes of a Stone Age boy, in Peter Dickinson's books (e.g., *The Weathermonger*) readers see values in a new perspective because the stories are set in an imaginary period when society has turned against everything mechanical and has gone back several centuries in its ways of living—and thinking. Myths and legends from this and other lands can, if they are well retold, also serve to distance problems and 8—11 year olds will move very naturally from discussing details of the story to talking about their own situation.

The discussions which arise when pupils have become engrossed in a story are usually conducted at a much more profound level than those which are initiated in other ways. Concepts like right and wrong, conflict of loyalties, freedom, conscience, reconciliation, are all important in the

Middle school years and above, but the limited experience of the pupils makes it all too easy for discussions to become arguments in which positions are polarised and issues seen in black and white terms. Prejudices and half-understood opinions heard on the lips of adults are often used as battering rams to defeat opponents' views. It is quite a different exercise when the discussion can centre on detailed concrete illustrations and when the incidents being discussed are part of the shared experience of the whole class. It is impossible to decide in a vacuum whether a particular action is right or wrong; one needs to know the circumstances. The detail provided by a story makes it possible to discuss whether a particular action was right or wrong *in that situation*. Examples of the kind of story which is particularly useful in providing material out of which discussion can arise are: *The Diddakoi* by Rumer Godden, *I am David* by Anne Holm, *The Dolphin Crossing* by Jill Paton Walsh, *Lord of the Flies* by William Golding, *The Cay* by Theodore Taylor, *The Wizard of Earthsea* by Ursula Le Guin, *To Kill a Mocking Bird* by Harper Lee, the musical *West Side Story* and, for senior pupils, *Red Shift* by Alan Garner, Robert Bolt's play about Sir Thomas More *A Man for All Seasons* and *The Plague* by Albert Camus.

Secondary teachers with only one or two periods a week for religious education may be feeling that the time needed for reading and discussing a book is a luxury they cannot afford. Cooperation with the English department however could mean that when a suitable book is being read in the English lessons the religious education teacher could use his more limited time for discussion arising out of the story—assuming, of course, that he knows the book well himself and that he keeps in touch with the English teacher both to discover which sections have captured the imagination of the pupils and to avoid repeating the kind of discussions which have taken place in English. Even if cooperation with the English department proves impossible it is still worth using some religious education time for reading and discussing literature. The resulting discussion will be so much less superficial than that which normally takes place around the familiar topics in the syllabus—personal relationships, use of money, loneliness, old age, etc.

If we return to the criteria which were suggested on p.28 for those activities which make a contribution to the implicit element in religious education we shall see that what we have been considering so far in this chapter meets some of the criteria—helping pupils to understand themselves and other people better and helping them to understand better their relationship to other people. What about the rest of the criteria?

Literature makes a smaller, though not a negligible, contribution towards helping the pupils to understand the natural world and their relationship to it. It happens incidentally in stories which deal with living growing things (e.g., *Joseph's Yard* by Charles Keeping, *Johan's Year* by Inger and Lasse Sandberg), or where the natural setting of the story—sea or forest or prairie—is sensitively handled (e.g., *The Little House in the Big Woods* by Laura Ingalls Wilder, *The Boy who was Afraid* by Armstrong Sperry, *A Stranger at Green Knowe* by L. M. Boston, *The Cay* by Theodore Taylor). It happens more directly in stories that deal with some form of natural disaster (e.g., *Avalanche* by A. Rutgers Van der Loeff, *Hills End* by Ivan Southall). And it happens in books which describe wild life (e.g., *A Zoo in my Luggage* by Gerald Durrell, *A Ring of Bright Water* by Gavin Maxwell).

However, it is to the last of the criteria—raising questions about human experience and about the mystery of what it is to be human—that literature makes a contribution for which there is really no adequate substitute.

Man is a dreamer. His feet may be planted firmly on this solid earth, his everyday life may be mundane and prosaic, but he refuses to believe that there is nothing more. In his dreams he catches a glimpse of a world of magic and mystery which beckons him on, and the vision refreshes him and gives him new strength for his everyday life.

To experience this world of enchantment is both natural and necessary for children, and literature can be the means of entering it. There are many stories of fantasy for young children, but in such books as Rumer Godden's *The Mousewife* and Mary Norton's *The Borrowers* children are introduced to a wistful yearning, a longing for something that is only glimpsed and not fully understood. The Mousewife senses it through her friendship with the caged dove, and Arrietty as she peers out at a tiny part of the garden through the grating from the enclosed world of the Borrowers under the kitchen floor. For slightly older children it is encountered in a book like Henry Treece's *The Dream-Time*, set in prehistoric days, where the crippled boy longs for a world where making beautiful things is thought to be more important than fighting.

Some stories are set in this other world. Books life J.R.R. Tolkien's *The Hobbit* and C. S. Lewis's *The Lion, the Witch and the Wardrobe* and the other Narnia stories transport the reader into a land that is strange and yet at the same time familiar. Such books explore some of the most potent motifs in human experience—the journey, the quest and the conflict between good and evil. These motifs are expressions of man's deep-seated belief that human life is not something that can ever be static, complete, self-contained. Man is an 'unfinished' creature; he is always in process of 'becoming'. To be called ever onward, in the quest for something that is infinitely precious and that is worth making great sacrifices for, and to respond to that call, is what it is to be human. Within any religious tradition the call and the quest and the goal are seen as related to that ultimate reality, however they name it, that men worship, but the recognition of the quest is not the prerogative only of religious people. It is the heritage of all men, by virtue of their humanity.

It is in myths and legends that these themes are most extensively explored, and this kind of literature has an important role to play in the Middle school years. There is a list of myths and legends on pp.195—6.

We must say something here about terminology. There is no agreement among scholars about the precise meanings of 'myth' and 'legend', and a quick glance at the library shelves is enough to show that the collectors of myths, legends, folk tales and fairy tales sit lightly to any systematic classification. It is perfectly true that the boundaries between these different kinds of writing cannot be drawn with any precision, but it is perhaps helpful to keep the word 'legend' for stories which had some basis in history or which could have had a basis in history, even though many of the details—monsters, supernatural powers, etc.—move beyond the historical. Legends tend to describe 'miraculous' events in an otherwise recognisable world of men and women, kings and warriors, voyages and battles, whether against human enemies or against monsters. Myths, on the other hand, move right out of our world and can be peopled by gods, demons, the elements, sun, moon and stars as well as by men and women (very seldom by children!).

Legends certainly explore the motifs referred to above—the journey, the quest and the conflict between good and evil (e.g., the Grail stories)— and they express man's sense that there are heroic deeds to be done, ordeals to be endured, threatening forces to be outwitted or overcome (e.g., the stories of Theseus or of Beowulf), but myths express an even more basic awareness of what is involved in man's existence. Myths are the stories men live by. Of course the concept of myth is much wider than stories from ancient times. Any country or cohesive group of people has its own potent myths in the light of which it interprets its actions. (One of the most obvious examples in this century was the Nazi 'Aryan myth'.) However, in the context of using literature in religious education we are restricting our attention to the stories which have come down to us from the early days of a people's existence. It is these that seem to have a universal appeal, to be able to speak to men across the ages, and to communicate at a deeper level than other stories. Myths express what is significant in man's experience.

Myths should never be treated as merely pre-scientific attempts to explain how things began. This would be to regard them as equivalent to our modern scientific explanations, with the implication that now that we actually know why, for example, it is dark at night and light in the daytime, or what the sky is 'made of', we hardly need primitive man's 'explanation'. This patronising attitude to myths from the vantage point of our scientific age misses altogether their real significance. It is true that primitive man was probably fascinated by origins, by how things began, but he did not create myths primarily to satisfy his 'scientific' curiosity. Their creation met a much more profound and basic need. It was one of the ways in which man came to terms with his experience, and expressed his response both to the elemental forces by which he found himself surrounded and to the powers, partly within himself and partly outside himself, which played such an important if largely inexplicable part in his life (e.g., the myth of Prometheus, or of the death of Baldur).

If we just present one or two myths to children and leave it at that it may well mean that they see little significance in the stories. A more useful way is to take, for example, a series of creation myths from different parts of the world. If the children are helped to see that all these stories came out of early man's experience, they can find elements that the myths have in common, no matter how diverse the actual stories—elements such as conflict, good and evil, the establishment of order out of chaos, etc. They will then be able to see that although the myths are not 'true' in the sense that the events actually happened, they are 'true to man's experience'.

It is for this reason that the normal kind of class discussion is far less valuable as a follow-up to the reading or telling of myths than an attempt to express through the creative arts something of what the pupils feel the myths to be saying. The working out of a ritual dance, the creation of music to accompany it, the making and wearing of masks, the designing of a symbolic frieze, the writing of poetry—all these can be effective ways of 'saying' what cannot be expressed adequately through ordinary language. Primitive man was trying to communicate something about experiences which could not be captured and neatly analysed. He was 'feeling' more than 'thinking'. If a myth is to communicate anything to us today then the appropriate response will not be an intellectual discussion. It will be a response that involves the whole of us, a response in which we enter into the experiences which are the substance of the myth, and 'feel', for example, the cosmic struggle between light and darkness.

At a later stage in their schooling pupils will need to look at the part that myth plays in religion. If they are to gain any real understanding of the significance of myth they must have 'felt' as well as thought what myths are about, and the best preparation for that is this kind of encounter with myths within the implicit element in religious education during the Middle school years.

8

Other men's faiths

Now we come to the explicit side of religious education and we begin by considering how we should approach the teaching of other faiths.

The discarding of the old set of initials, C.S.R. (Comparative Study of Religions), is not without significance. The method most frequently followed in the C.S.R. courses in fifth and sixth forms was to select certain major religions and set them alongside each other, devoting a few lessons to each. As the name implies the religions were compared, or, more accurately, contrasted, and the emphasis was put on the beliefs and practices which distinguished them from each other—and from Christianity.

The purpose of teaching world religions now is certainly not to gloss over differences or to pretend that all religions are virtually the same, but it does seek to show that the religious quest is common to mankind and that certain elements, e.g., worship, sacred places, sacred writings, beliefs about the significance of man, etc., are found in most religions even if they are expressed in diverse ways. The emphasis is on what unites men rather than on what divides them.

Although the study of other religions is now an indispensable element in religious education, this does not mean that Christianity is to be replaced by the teaching of other faiths. Nor does it mean, as it is sometimes claimed, that equal time must be given to each religion. Even if religious education had a great deal more time at its disposal than is usually allocated to it, a syllabus divided equally among several religions would result in a very superficial understanding of what religion is. Part of our aim is to help pupils to understand what it would mean to take a religion seriously and this can be achieved only if they are able to explore at least one religion fairly thoroughly. This will naturally be the dominant religion (or religions) of the country in which the pupils live. 'Dominant' here does not mean powerful or large, it means having contributed significantly to the nation's cultural heritage.

A religion can be studied most effectively only within its cultural context. In this country it is Christianity that has shaped much of our cultural heritage. The Christian Church is part of our community and has been involved in our history, many of the values in our society owe their origin to the Judaeo-Christian tradition, and the Bible has had a formative role in the field of art and music as well as of literature and language. The teacher has access to so much more material about the Christian religion than about other faiths. This is not a reference merely to R.E. textbooks and other sources of information about religions. It refers rather to the infinite number of illustrations, some brief, some in considerable detail, which can be found in history, literature, music, painting, sculpture, etc. It also refers to the fact that the pupils can study at first hand the significance of the religion in the life of its adherents and the different ways in which it is expressed, indirectly as well as directly, in the life of the nation.

It is by no means being disputed that pupils who happen to live in an area where there is a Hindu community can gain a valuable understanding of, let us say, the festival of Divali. This should certainly form part of their religious education. But however careful their study, they will in the end have gained only a limited insight into what the festival really means in the life of the people of India.

We can perhaps illustrate this by reversing the situation and imagining a class of children in a town in India studying the Christian festival of Christmas as it is being observed by a number of English families who happen to live there. The Indian children would learn about presents and family parties and decorations and (artificial) Christmas trees. They might attend a Christmas service in the unpretentious building that the small English community use for a church. They would hear the story of a baby called Jesus who was born in a stable a long time ago, and from the English children they would hear of a man called Santa Claus (dressed most unsuitably for the Indian climate) who brings presents to children (though not apparently to Hindu children). The Indian class would probably have some difficulty in fitting their various pieces of information into any kind of coherent pattern, but even more important, they would not have experienced all those other things which go to make the festival significant in the life of the people of Britain—the festive air that pervades the whole community, Christmas cards everywhere, extra postal deliveries, street decorations, crowded shops, the chance of meeting Santa Claus in a department store, carol singing, school parties and concerts, Christmas programmes on radio and television, and a national holiday on Christmas Day.

The logic of the position which has been outlined is that if a school in, say, Pakistan had similar religious education aims and wanted to help its pupils to understand the nature of religion, it would of course introduce them to the main features of other living faiths but it would explore those features at greatest depth in Islam. Similarly, the religion to be studied most thoroughly in Israel would be Judaism.

This central place given to Christianity in our schools may make some teachers rejoice that they can apparently go on teaching the Christian faith, and fill others with horror that we seem to be back with traditional R.E. However, neither assumption would be right because, even though Christianity plays a larger part in the syllabus than other religions, we now have to approach it in a completely different way. In traditional R.E. it was taught 'from the inside', within a context of commitment. The truth of the Christian faith was taken for granted and pupils learned stories from its scriptures, sections of its history, the lives of some of its important adherents, the main festivals of the Church's year and fragments of its theology. It was assumed that the pupils were, or should be, Christians. (Notice how many R.E. textbooks use the pronoun 'we' when referring to Christian beliefs and ways of acting.)

A context of commitment is absolutely right within a religious community. Children growing up in a faith are taught about it 'from inside'. But a school is in a completely different situation. Its task is not to teach for belief or to initiate children or young people into a particular religious tradition. That is the role of the voluntary religious community— the Church, the Synagogue, the Mosque—and the religious family.

The issue becomes acute where there are children of other faiths in the school, and sensitive teachers have long been uneasy about a form of religious education that had little to distinguish it from what some of the children were receiving in their Sunday School or Junior Church. But it is not a question only for the multi-faith school. Even where there are no adherents of other religions in a locality it would be surprising indeed if there were no humanist families, and that in itself creates a pluralist situation.

However, we are educating children for a wider community than the immediate locality. The schools are the community's schools and one of the main reasons for an educational rather than an evangelistic approach to religious education is that it is not honest to teach as truth in the community's schools beliefs over which opinion is divided in the community as a whole. A similar situation exists in relation to politics. The inclusion of political studies in the curriculum is more than justified in a democratic country; what could not be tolerated would be the presentation of the beliefs of one political party or ideology as the only right way to view society or effect political change.

Both religious and political studies raise questions about the teacher's own beliefs, and it has even been suggested that teachers should themselves be neutral. However, there is all the difference in the world between holding a neutral position oneself and maintaining a neutral attitude to what one is teaching. It does not matter how committed a teacher is to a set of beliefs or how active he is outside the school in trying to persuade others of their value and their truth so long as he maintains a professional approach within the school and does not betray his trust as an educationist by taking advantage of the fact that he has a captive audience.

Maintaining a neutral attitude to the material one is teaching does not mean that the teacher has to hide his own beliefs. He should certainly give them honestly if he is asked for them by his pupils, and there is no reason why he should not explain where he stands in relation to any issue that is being discussed, especially with older pupils.

What does an objective approach to the teaching of religions look like in practice?

In the first place it means quite simply a different way of introducing beliefs. Where, in traditional R.E., a teacher might have said, 'God was revealed in Jesus Christ' he would now say 'Christians believe that God was revealed in Jesus Christ' or, occasionally and where appropriate, 'I personally believe that . . .' (There will of course be many statements about which the teacher will have to say 'Many Christians believe . . .' or 'This Christian group believes'.) This is a very small change linguistically but it is a highly significant one. Those who have tried it have found that the change is easily made and that it quickly becomes a natural way of speaking—and one much appreciated by the pupils.

Secondly, the objective approach means being scrupulously fair in our selection and presentation of material. We must always compare best with best. We must not, for example, compare Christianity with

Hinduism by setting the Christian ideals of love and self-sacrifice and service over against the selfishness and exploitation and acceptance of social injustice that can be found in Indian society. Nor must we compare the two religions by setting the arrogance and the hypocrisy and the evils of the rat race that can be found in British society over against the lofty ideals of harmony and self-discipline of Hinduism. Every religion has its ideals and these are set before its adherents, but they are a summons to perfection, not a description of the behaviour of ordinary human beings endowed with a far from perfect human nature and caught in the pressures of a far from perfect society.

Thirdly, it means teaching about religions, and non-religious systems such as humanism and Marxism, in a way that their adherents would approve. This approach will be reflected in such details as the terminology we use. For instance, in teaching about Islam we shall never call it Muhammadanism (or Mohammedanism). As Muslims point out, this implies that the Muslim's faith is in Muhammad rather than in God. In teaching about Buddhism we shall use the name Theravada and not Hinayana, introducing the latter (which means 'lesser vehicle') only in the course of explaining how the adherents of Mahayana ('greater vehicle') used it to indicate the smaller number of people who could be carried to salvation by the teachings of the Theravada school of Buddhism. In teaching about Judaism we shall never call the Jewish Bible the 'Old Testament'. We may say that the Jewish Bible is the same as the Christian Old Testament (apart from the order of the books), but the very name 'Old Testament' (meaning old covenant) implies that the religion was only preparatory and that it has now been superseded—a judgment that no Jew could possibly accept.

Then there are conventions to be respected. Muslims never allow any representation of Muhammad. We shall therefore not ask our pupils to draw any picture of the Prophet. This is not just a negative avoidance of what would give offence, something which regretfully we feel we have to do. It has a positive value. As we explain to our pupils why they are not being asked to draw a picture of Muhammad we are helping them to understand something about Islam and the intensity of its feelings about the dangers of idolatry.

Fourthly, it involves refraining from making value judgments. Some of the families represented in the school will be convinced of the truth of Christianity. Other families may equally be convinced of the truth of

54

Judaism or Islam, or they may be convinced humanists. In no circumstances could it be the task of the school to adjudicate between them. And the principle applies equally when the school is not a multi-faith one.

The teaching of world religions makes great demands on the teacher. In addition to the extensive—and accurate—knowledge of other religions that is required, and the much more comprehensive knowledge of Christianity than was needed for traditional R.E., it also requires a high degree of sensitivity. As M. A. C. Warren wrote (*General Introduction to The Christian Presence* series, S.C.M. Press) 'Our first task in approaching another people, another culture, another religion, is to take off our shoes, for the place we are approaching is holy. Else we may find ourselves treading on men's dreams.'

A useful maxim for both teacher and pupil is never to say anything about a religion that one would not want to say in the presence of one of its adherents. This does not mean that we are restricted to fulsome eulogies or polite trivialities. It allows plenty of room for the expression of disagreement, but it ensures that the study will be conducted in an atmosphere of respect for other people, even where we cannot understand or identify with their beliefs.

One of our main aims in teaching about other religions is to help our pupils to stand where the believer stands, to see what his religion must look—and feel—like to him. And yet, in the last resort, this is impossible. To do it would mean actually being a believer. It is only within a commitment to a religion that its beliefs, rituals, worship, code of ethics really fall into place as parts of a coherent whole which expresses for the believer the 'real' and the 'true'. As teachers we are faced with the paradox that we are trying to help our pupils to understand what Hinduism looks— and feels—like to a Hindu, and yet at the same time we know that we can never fully achieve this.

Our concern with other religions takes on a new dimension when we have pupils of other faiths in the school. Wherever possible we should use them as resource persons. This not only gives a sense of reality to the study for the rest of the class but it can also increase the confidence of the young 'expert', who finds that instead of always being at the receiving end because so many things in our culture—and in the curri- culum of our schools—are strange to him, he has something to contri- bute, something to offer which the rest of the class needs.

It would of course be a mistake to assume that just because a person is an Indian he must be a Hindu or a Sikh. He may not have kept up his religion. (He may even be a Muslim or a Christian.) However, it is only in the Upper school units concerned with such things as the meaning of worship, or beliefs about life after death, or the study of a religion as a whole, that this will be significant, for what First and Middle school pupils will be learning about is as much cultural as religious.

While we are discussing the psychological needs of the pupils of other faiths we must remember that any migrant is likely to suffer from cultural shock. (This can affect even those who move from the north to the south of the same country.) Children from countries like Australia and New Zealand, whose race and religion are usually the same as those of the natives of their adopted country, still have to make many adjustments and it will, for example, be important for them to be able to explain to their classmates what it is like to have Christmas in the summer and Easter in the autumn.

Much more difficult are the adjustments which have to be made by children from the Caribbean. They are often Christians—and indeed they may practise their Christianity with a verve and a dedication such as is seldom shown by European Christians—but much in the culture of Britain may seem strange to them and in a country that is not free from racial prejudice they may well have to face discrimination. The sensitive teacher will be aware of the deprivation which children suffer when they are cut off from their cultural roots, and will try to compensate for it by 'recognising' the Caribbean culture, using some of its stories and having a topic on the islands from which the children (or their parents or grandparents) came.

This concern for the cultural shock suffered by those whose families have been migrants to this country strictly speaking takes us beyond the teaching of world religions. However, our attitude to pupils of other faiths is the same as our attitude to pupils from other cultural backgrounds an acceptance of and a respect for differences, and a willingness to give positive value to both the pupil and the culture from which he has come.

9

World religions — principles into practice

In recent years the teaching of world religions has become increasingly popular, but there has been a tendency to add it to the syllabus rather than to make it an integral part of religious education. In one sense this was inevitable as long as schools were working on the traditional type of syllabus, or even an experience-based one. Pupils might welcome the break that a course on other religions afforded but they would not be likely to see its relation to the biblical material or the themes or the discussions on personal relationships and homelessness that formed the staple diet of their R.E.

What then will the teaching of world religions look like if it is completely integrated into religious education and if it is contributing to the overall aim of helping pupils to understand the nature of religion?

The first point to be made is that in this as in all other aspects of the subject we shall be concerned to lay the right foundations and to build on them the kind of structure that enables the pupils gradually to extend their knowledge and their understanding. If we try to do too much too soon we invite misunderstanding and distortion. This is why the study of a religion as a whole should not be attempted in the First or Middle school years.

The most important of our foundation stones is an attitude of acceptance of, and respect for, other people. The study of world religions, at whatever age it is undertaken, will produce only negative results if the pupils are intolerant or defensive, and if they are unwilling to try to stand where another person stands and see how something must look to him. As we saw (chapters 4–7), the deepening of a pupil's understanding of himself and other people and the development of his own confidence (without which it is almost impossible for him to have a positive attitudes towards others) are part of the implicit element in R.E. and are achieved most effectively through the teacher's encouragement of sensitive relationships within the class and the extension of these positive attitudes to the wider community, and through the skilful use of literature.

At First school level this is where the emphasis must lie. For those First schools which have no children of other faiths the implicit element will probably comprise the whole of their preparation for the later study of world religions. Possible exceptions to this are the biblical background units which could be done with the seven to nine age groups (see pp.91 f.). Although these units are part of the study of Christianity they also provide an introduction to important aspects of Judaism.

Where the First school is fortunate enough to have children from different religious communities there will be many opportunities for direct reference to the relevant religions. These will not of course be formal lessons or schemes of work. They will be mainly incidental, arising perhaps from the arrival of a new member of the class or from the celebration of a festival or from the casual comment or item of news contributed by a child. The teacher's role is first and foremost to be a willing listener, but it also includes helping the other children in the class to understand and to be interested in the contribution. Where, for example, a small girl wants to share the fact that she has been given a new sari, the teacher might arrange for the rest of the class to learn how a sari is put on. This would capture the imagination of the girls and it would probably provide an interesting variant in their dressing-up games and perhaps feature in their paintings. It would thus have been successful in two ways: in developing a positive attitude of interest and appreciation among the non-Indian children, and in increasing the Indian children's confidence and sense of significance.

A sharing of occasions, a willingness to accept and respect differences, and an acknowledgement of the sincerity of those whose practices are not the same as ours, will be important at all ages. Even in the Middle school years and above, an indirect approach may be an essential preparation for any direct study of other religions. In situations where there is racial tension or the expression of intolerance towards particular religious communities, the tackling of the very questions which are causing bitterness in the community is more likely to lead to confirmation of prejudices. Children are influenced by their parents' attitudes and where there are emotional elements in a situation so close to the children's experience prejudices ('pre-judgments') are unfortunately not removed by rational argument.

Prejudices based on stereotypes of ethnic groups can be found, especially among 12—15 year olds, even where there are no representatives of those groups in the area, and teachers have to be sensitive to the possible existence of such prejudices before embarking on a study of the corresponding religion.

This is unfortunately particularly acute in relation to Judaism. We have not been sufficiently alert to this problem, nor have we been sufficiently aware of the way in which traditional R.E., both in the school and in the Church, has contributed (albeit unintentionally) to anti-Semitism. Teaching about the origins of Christianity is of course teaching about a situation in which there was conflict and rejection—on both sides, but it is crucial that we should think out how we can teach positively about one religion without encouraging negative (and un-Christian) attitudes to another.

The fact that it is all too easy not to notice conflict of aims in our teaching was illustrated by the young teacher in London who was exercised about a current outburst of anti-Semitism in the area. She decided to introduce a discussion on the subject one day with her 14 year olds and, knowing how sensitive the topic was, she prepared the lesson with great thoroughness. However, she was completely unaware of the incongruity that existed between her lesson with the 14 year olds and her lesson two periods earlier with some 11 year olds. The younger pupils were working through the Acts of the Apostles. They had written a play about the stoning of Stephen and they acted it with vigour and evident enthusiasm. There was no doubt about who the villains were—the Jews!

Assuming that the attitude of our pupils is not such as to preclude a direct study of other religions, how do we decide which ones to select?

In areas where there are adherents of other faiths these religions will have priority. One can extend this principle to say that the five major religions represented in Britain—Christianity, Hinduism, Islam, Judaism and Sikhism—obviously have a strong claim to be considered. Even where the pupils do not encounter members of the last four of these faiths in their ordinary everyday life, they may well do so through television programmes or when they visit large towns or cities. And they could easily find themselves in the situation of the secondary school in a rural area which suddenly met Islam in the person of a 14 year old Asian girl whose family had been expelled from Uganda.

What about the other great world faith, Buddhism? In the Middle
school years it is possible to draw on Buddhism for the unit 'Sacred
Places' because there are plenty of books, slides, filmstrips, etc., available,
and the characteristic architecture of Buddhist temples and stupas and
the images of the Buddha in the former are visually attractive and they
add to the value of the unit—showing the variety and yet universality of
sacred places, without having to introduce the pupils to the abstract
beliefs of Buddhism.

There is less reason to draw on Buddhism for the unit 'Festivals' (see
p.70), but towards the end of the unit 'Signs and Symbols' one might
well introduce two Buddhist symbols: the lotus, rising pure and unstained
from the muddy waters in which it has grown, and the twelve-spoked
wheel of life, representing the endless round of rebirths to which man
is tied and from which he longs to escape. These would be only brief
references to the beliefs for the emphasis would be on the actual symbols,
but they would serve as a useful introduction to central ideas in Buddhism.
They would constitute part of the contribution which the pupils would
be able to bring to their more detailed study of the Buddhist understanding
of man in the unit 'What is Man?'

The pupils would also learn something about Buddhism in the unit
'Sacred Writings'. Although it would not be necessary to devote a great
deal of time to Buddhist Scriptures, the contrast between the sacred
writings of Theravada and Mahayana Buddhism is significant and provides
an illustration which cannot easily be paralleled in other religions. In
addition there are some passages, especially poems and extracts from the
'Questions of King Milinda' which depict aspects of Buddhist teaching
in a form that is relatively easy to understand (see especially the poem
'The Rhinoceros' and the passage in the 'Questions of King Milinda'
where the monk Nagasena uses the illustration of the chariot to demonstrate that there is no such thing as the self. They can be found in
Buddhist Scriptures edited by Edward Conze and published by Penguin).
Pupils should meet passages like these in whichever of the two units they
do first, 'What is Man?' or 'Sacred Writings', and they will then be able to
use them when they come to the other unit.

In this way the pupil's encounter with Buddhism is carefully phased
so that at sixth form level he is able to tackle a more comprehensive
study of the religion without the danger of the frightening distortions
and over-simplifications which can result when 13 and 14 year olds are

given a series of lessons on a religion whose concepts are so difficult for a westerner to grasp. In addition he will be able to study such developments as Zen Buddhism, which is in some ways a complete antithesis to Theravada Buddhism, without becoming completely confused.

Nothing has been said so far about primal religions—that much neglected sector of the world religions field. Partly because resource material is so scarce and partly because of the traditional European assumption that primal religions are somehow infantile expressions of religion and therefore not worth bothering about (the two reasons are no doubt linked), it is not easy for the teacher to include them in the religious education syllabus. There are however myths and other stories from the Pacific Islands and from the African countries which can be used with the 7—13 age group, and in view of the general neglect of primal religions it is important that we should include them.

Primal religions will come most significantly into the Upper school units dealing with ultimate questions, particularly 'What is Man?'. John V. Taylor's book *The Primal Vision* (Christian Presence series, S.C.M. Press, 1963) is especially relevant here. It sets out clearly and compellingly some of the values that the Western world could well learn from the African's understanding of the nature of man.

Primal religions will feature again in the sixth form unit 'The Study of Religion', but great care has to be taken here over the selection of resource material. Well-known books such as Frazer's *Golden Bough* are excellent as illustrations of a particular method of study and of the presuppositions which Frazer and other anthropologists of the period brought to their studies, but they are extremely dangerous if the pupils think that they are source books for contemporary anthropological thinking. Such books are likely to reinforce stereotypes about primal religions, but a course which gives sixth formers some insight into both the history of the study of religion during the last century and its current methods and concerns will, in the process, have done much to restore the primal religions to the position they deserve.

For the units dealing with ultimate questions it would be both time-consuming and monotonous to work through every major religion as well as humanism and Marxism in every unit. In selecting religions the teacher will take two main factors into consideration: the religions which the pupils have encountered in their earlier studies, which will form an important part of what they can contribute to this new area of study, and the religions (and non-religious systems of belief) in whose teachings the topics are particularly significant.

For instance, for 'What is Man?' he will include Christianity, partly because, if Christianity is the religion which is being studied at greatest depth, it will always be included, but also because it is a religion in which the doctrine of man holds a central place. He will certainly include humanism because man is the key concept in humanism. He will possibly include Marxism because, although Marxism has little to say about man as an individual, it has significant beliefs about man in society and about the destiny of mankind. He will want his pupils to consider the question: Does it make any difference to what you believe about man if you believe that there is only one God? So he will include some comparison of Christian, Muslim and Jewish ideas with those of the Indian religious traditions.

For the unit 'Suffering' he will include Buddhism because suffering is the key concept in Buddhism. He will include Christianity, not only because it will always form part of the study but because suffering is a key concept in Christianity—the Cross lies at the heart of the Christian faith. He will include humanism because it is important to discover how people who believe that there is no power or purpose greater than man come to terms with suffering. It will not be necessary to include Marxism because it would have little that is distinctive to add to humanist beliefs. Some place should be given to Judaism because of the actual suffering that has been the lot of Jews through history and because of the way in which they have interpreted it, but Hinduism, Islam and probably Sikhism could be left out. This is not to suggest that there is nothing in these religions about suffering, but the R.E. teacher's time allocation means that he frequently has to look for the minimum amount of material that will enable him to achieve the aim of a series of lessons. He will also want to avoid the danger of superficiality.

There are of course religions other than those which have been mentioned. They will probably not play a major part in religious education in this country, but teachers may want to draw on them for specific purposes, e.g., Confucianism for its Five Classics (in 'Sacred Writings') or for its ethical system, Shinto for its association of state and religion, Jainism for its reverence for life, Zoroastrianism if senior pupils are studying the astonishing flowering of religion across the world in the eighth to fifth centuries B.C.

The selection of aspects of a religion has to be handled with extreme care. It can very easily degenerate into a 'bits and pieces' method. There are a number of dangers to be avoided.

First, many beliefs and practices can be understood only within the wider context of the religion. In that case we must either not use such illustrations, or we must make certain that our pupils have sufficient background knowledge to understand them without distortion. One R.E. textbook deals with the subject of Birth in just under 400 words, referring to the customs of seven peoples, apparently chosen at random (Eskimo, Sherpa, Yoruba, Ibo, Australian aborigine, Navaho Indian and Hebrew). And the passage describes for three of these groups practices involving the killing of babies! This is a reversion to what has been called the 'rag-bag' approach of anthropologists of half a century ago. It does not do justice to the peoples whose customs are presented in isolation from their whole way of life, nor does it tackle the subject with sufficient thoroughness.

Secondly, and closely related to the previous point, is the problem that there is seldom a straightforward transfer of ideas from one religion to another. Pupils will be seriously misled if they are allowed to think that, e.g., when the Hindu uses the word *avatar* (incarnation) he means what the Christian means by 'incarnation', or that the Buddhist *nirvana* is like the Christian 'heaven', or that 'reincarnation' means exactly the same thing in Buddhism as it means in Hinduism. This is a danger that one has to be on one's guard against in any teaching of world religions but it is particularly likely to arise when attention is being focussed on apparently similar ideas in several religions.

Thirdly, many beliefs and practices are not characteristic of a religion as a whole, and when that is the case we must make it clear. It is no more possible to say 'Hindus believe' about much of that religion than it is possible to say 'Christians believe'. Christians, for example, may have quite different views on such things as infant baptism, the literal truth of the Bible, sacramental confession, abstaining from alchohol and the Second Coming. This problem, again, is not peculiar to the studying of selected religious phenomena. It is also a danger when a religion is studied as a whole, a danger that is accentuated by the books, often designed for use in school, which treat each religion so briefly that they are not able to do more than give generalised summaries.

Fourthly, religions do not remain unchanged through the centuries and if we want to use illustrations from the past we must make it clear that they no longer apply today. Judaism is the religion that suffers most in this respect. Some courses on worship prepared for secondary schools have included in the section on Judaism the Temple and the sacrificial system! Other teachers choose their material for other religions from the present but go only to the Bible for Christianity.

It may be reassuring to some teachers to learn that although we always have to be alert to the dangers outlined above, the units suggested for the Middle school years have fewer pitfalls than those which older pupils might tackle.

So far we have made no reference to teaching about the founders of religions. R.E. syllabuses and books for schools tend to introduce a religion with an account of the life of the founder, and the lives of founders are frequently suggested for the under elevens. However, both these approaches must be questioned.

In the first place, children of Junior school age are interested in practical activity. They enjoy learning about people who do things; they are far less interested in people whose importance lies in their teachings.

Secondly, the significance of a founder can be grasped only when his life and teaching can be seen in the context of the religious situation in which he grew up, with the complex relationship between his reaction to it and its influence on him.

Thirdly, because new religions do not appear in a vacuum but emerge from existing religions there is bound to be an element of conflict. A book for children on the life of Guru Nanak emphasised his concern for peace and goodwill to all men, but the Muslims of his time were portrayed in such a way as to discourage an attitude of goodwill towards them! More familiar to us will be the stories of the life and teaching of Jesus, which involve conflict with Judaism. (It was a six year old who said 'Poor Jesus, he got nails in his feet. The Jews did it.')

It is for these reasons that any extended reference to founders of religions is best done in the thirteen-plus years (but see chapter 14 for teaching about Jesus). Even for these older pupils, however, the life of the founder is not the most effective way to introduce pupils to a religion (for Hinduism and Judaism it is actually impossible). The tendency to start at the beginning and work through chronologically is deep-seated in the English education system, but it is a tendency that needs to be questioned. There are times, especially in higher education, when it is an appropriate method but in the field of religion what matters most, both for the subject and to the pupils, is the living religion as it is practised today. Some aspect of this is therefore an effective way in to the study of a religion. It will soon become obvious that one has to go back in time, particularly to the founder, if one is to understand the religion properly, but it is the pupils' own discovery that this extension of their study is necessary that is the most important part of what we are trying to achieve.

For pupils whose R.E. has followed a pattern similar to that suggested in this book, the study of a religion as a whole in the Upper school years is not unduly difficult, but where teachers are having to introduce world religions without having been able to lay the appropriate foundations there is plenty of scope for unsatisfying if not disastrous results. In such circumstances any unit should begin at a concrete level, with what is involved in actually being a Hindu, rather than with the intellectual beliefs of the religion. While this is appropriate for all levels of ability it is absolutely essential for the less able pupils.

A class of 13 year olds whose academic ability was slight and whose enthusiasm for R.E. was non-existent were transformed when they began a study of Islam. They copied pictures of mosques. They wrote out (in Arabic and English) Muslim prayers, the Sura of Unity, the Five Pillars of Islam, etc. They reproduced examples of Muslim art and architecture. They found out about the mosque, the Qur'an and Ramadan. They adored writing in Arabic, and their powers of concentration and the high standard of what they produced were a revelation to their teacher. At the end of the study when their work was carefully mounted and put on display for the rest of the school to see they were bursting with pride. Their course bore little relation to the conventional pattern—the life of the founder and the main beliefs and practices—but they had met most of the key concepts in Islam, the emphasis put on Arabic reflected quite accurately the importance of the language in Islam, and they had developed an enthusiasm which would be invaluable for later study.

Finally, a word about inviting the adherents of other faiths into the classroom. Where this is possible it is excellent, but the visit should be integrated into the class's study and the visitor should not just be asked to 'talk about his religion'. To communicate anything as complex as a religious faith, especially in a short talk, is a skilled task and the ordinary member of another faith is no more likely to be adept at it than his Christian counterpart would be.

Any systematic attempt at the exposition of a religion's beliefs is bound to be too difficult for children of First or Middle school age. It would indeed be ironic if, just as we had reached the conclusion that we should not try to teach Christian theology to this age group, our enthusiasm for world religions led us to attempt the even more impossible task of teaching the beliefs of other religions. Pupils should have thought out questions to put to the visitor so that what he says is directly related to the work they have been doing. However, particularly for younger children the most important thing will be the opportunity to meet the visitor and establish a relationship with him. Such an experience is a useful reminder that in studying religions we are studying not abstract belief systems but the living faith of men.

10

Festivals...

This chapter could just as well be called Celebration because it is about
a fundamental human characteristic which finds expression not only in
the patterns of festivals in the world's religions but also in a much wider
series of experiences—in families and in local communities and nations,
in spontaneous acts of celebration as well as in formalised rituals. Man
is a celebrating animal.

In Britain our Puritan heritage has done much to suppress this urge
to celebration (it is not without significance that we come low in the list
of European countries for the number of national holidays we have),
but for our children it is still a natural expression of joy and delight in
life.

Celebration is a way of saying Yes to the universe. This is not to
ignore tragedy, but rather to include it in a larger whole. It is an affirmation that tragedy is not the final word. Celebration is not just a form
of escapism in which we temporarily forget the problems of everyday
life. It does to a certain extent serve this purpose, particularly for those
people whose lives consist of grinding poverty, unremitting toil and a
constant struggle against hardship and suffering, but far from being a
frivolous avoidance of reality, it is a way of taking life seriously and
affirming its significance.

This affirmation of significance is probably seen most clearly in the
celebration of birth. It includes thanksgiving for the safety of mother
and child, but it is also the recognition of the beginning of a new life,
with all the promise that it holds. Beginnings are important reasons for
celebration (cf. marriage), and birthdays mark not just the passage of
time but the beginning of a new stage in life.

Celebration is also a way of saying that we belong together. It is
something that we do with other people. To celebrate on one's own is
a hollow activity. The continued celebration of birthdays through life
tends to happen mainly within families—and children and young people

who are concerned for elderly people who have to spend Christmas alone might also give serious thought to the sadness that is often felt when birthdays pass unnoticed by anyone.

Dance and music often accompany celebration, though the universal feature is probably food. The sharing of a common meal has always been a significant act, which expresses in symbolic form our common humanity.

Finding out about festivals will be an important part of religious education but it is essential that the pupils should experience celebration and not only learn about it. Primary schools already provide many such opportunities, and Infant schools are particularly good at making possible the spontaneous act of celebration. Children need both kinds of experience—the sheer expression of enjoyment and delight at something that has happened, and the careful preparations, the thrill of anticipation and the security of the familiar ritual which characterise the special occasion.

We turn now from the implicit side of religious education—the experiencing of celebration, to the explicit side.

Attention in the past has been focussed on Christmas and Easter, and they will still be important. They are part of the general cultural pattern of the country as well as of the faith of the Christian Church. In Chapter 11 we shall look at the specific problems relating to the way in which we handle them in school, but first let us look at the question of religious festivals in general.

Where there are pupils of other faiths in the school it is possible—indeed essential—to make explicit reference to the festivals of those faiths at a much earlier age than would otherwise be appropriate. They will be acknowledged and talked about, not because we are trying to teach about world religions but because the occasions are important in the lives of the children concerned. Schools recognise the festivals which are important in the lives of the English children, and this recognition must not be denied to those children for whom Christmas and Easter do not happen to be the 'high days and holidays' of their year.

For pupils of all ages, but especially for the youngest ones, it is important that they should be able to talk about their festivals. For the under elevens this will mean an account of what happens—what the festival means to the child himself, and not an objective description of its origin, history and religious significance. Our traditional obsession with history and theology is reflected in the fact that few of the books written for use in schools actually bring the festivals to life or show what they mean to those who celebrate them. Most accounts of the Jewish festival of Chanukah, for instance, devote most of their space to the historical origin of the festival in Judas Maccabaeus' time, and seldom go further in explaining what this essentially children's festival is like for the Jewish child today than describing the lighting of the candles on the successive days of the feast. This is not to deny the importance of the origin of the festival—and learning about it in the Middle school years will be a significant part of religious education—but just as important, and coming before the historical study, is learning about the festival in the lives of those who celebrate it.

Good resource material is as yet not easily available and it is certainly more expensive than the normal school can afford. Some teachers' centres have materials which can be borrowed for a period, but there are also ways in which a teacher can build up a useful collection. Families will almost certainly be willing to contribute Jewish New Year cards, Muslim Eid cards and Hindu Divali cards—not to mention Christian Christmas cards, when they have finished with them. Magazines and colour supplements carry illustrated articles from time to time on religions and their festivals. Calendars, and even advertisements, may prove useful; national airlines sometimes feature customs of the religion of their country. Where other faiths are represented in an area it may well be possible for the children, or adult members of the religious community, to bring to school objects associated with a festival.

It is important that we should use the children themselves as far as possible for information about the festivals of their religion. For the youngest ones this will mean, as we suggested above, just sharing with the teacher and with the rest of the class something of what the occasion means to them—parties, new clothes, special food, going with their families to the Synagogue or the Temple. For pupils of Middle school age and above, it can mean, in addition, explaining something about the background of the festival and perhaps how it is celebrated in the country where it is part of the culture of the nation as a whole. We shall not, of course, assume that our pupils will have all this information at their finger-tips. Many of them will have been born in this country and will not have experienced the festivals in the land from which their parents or grandparents came. And we shall no more expect the younger members of other faiths to be able to give a scholarly account of their religion than we would expect English children and young people to be able to give a scholarly account of Christianity. However, they will probably be only too willing to get information from their families or from other members of the religious community.

In addition to recognising those festivals which are significant for our pupils as they occur during the year, there are numerous ways in which festivals will figure in religious education. They will certainly find a place in the study of a religion as a whole in the Upper school years, and probably also in the unit 'Worship'. Festivals are one of the aspects of religious education most easily linked with other areas of study and our approach should therefore be particularly flexible.

In the First school years the only festivals apart from Christmas and Easter which will be included will be those which are observed locally. In the Middle schools years it is possible to extend the list. If a class is doing a study of the Festivals of Light (see p.156; not to be confused with campaigns to fight permissiveness in society!) the most likely religions will be Christianity, Judaism, Hinduism and Sikhism. A more general study of festivals will add Islam to the list.

Some teachers might have a particular reason for including Buddhism but apart from that there is less reason for including it here. This is only partly because pupils are unlikely to find the festivals being observed in Britain in the way in which they can find the festivals of the 'big five'. It is more because festivals do not play as prominent a part in Theravada Buddhism as they play in the other world religions, and although more emphasis is placed on festivals in some forms of Mahayana Buddhism, e.g., Tantrayana (Tibetan Buddhism) or the Japanese Pure Land sects, we would not be being true to the religion if we just selected examples from these very different Mahayana schools and presented them simply as 'Buddhist'. And yet if we tried to put them into their right setting, we should find ourselves involved in a great deal of explanation and extra teaching which would distract us from our main aim in this particular study.

The criteria for handling other men's religions, outlined in the two previous chapters, will of course also apply here. And we shall be particularly careful not to compare the contemporary observance of the festivals of one religion with the earlier form of those of another. There must be generations of school children for whom the Jewish Passover means a visit to the Temple at Jerusalem and the sacrificing of the Passover lambs!

There is certainly a place in religious education for finding out about festivals which were once celebrated differently, and even festivals which no longer exist in any form, such as those of the religions of Greece and Rome and the ancient Near East. Some of the ancient harvest festivals may usefully be set alongside modern ones as an illustration of the significant part that the return of the seasons plays in the life of man. What matters is that the pupils should have quite clear ideas about what it is that they are studying.

We began this chapter by talking about celebration as a basic human experience and about the importance of the children's own experience of celebration as part of the implicit element in religious education. While the festivals of the major religions will form a large part of the explicit side, we must not give our pupils the impression that festivals belong only within religions. We shall be concerned to let them explore the concept of man as a celebrating animal. In the Middle school years and above this may be the main aim of a particular unit, but it will always be the context in which we set any study of festivals. For even the youngest children a human experience theme like 'Parties' will cover the range of parties within their experience. At this age the children themselves make no distinction between parties associated with occasions like birthdays and parties associated with religious occasions such as Christmas or the ending of the Muslim Fast of Ramadan. This inclusive approach is absolutely right and natural, and we should be less anxious than we often are with older age groups to draw a clear line between 'religious' and 'non-religious' celebrations. Within religions celebration will be expressed in forms that reflect the significant beliefs of the faith but the fact that the boundary lines are blurred is perhaps illustrated most clearly in this country by the festival of Christmas.

What is demanded of the teacher in the handling of festivals is clear thinking about the nature of the material and the aims of the study, and the realisation that religious festivals are an expression of a very deep-seated human characteristic.

11

...Christmas and Easter

Christmas is so firmly established in the primary school year that it would be difficult to visualise the autumn term without it, and although Easter does not dominate the spring term to the same extent there are many teachers who feel that whatever else they do they must tell their children the stories from the Gospels about Jesus' death and resurrection.

The actual festivals always fall during the school holidays and so are not really part of the school year at all, but the prominent place given in religious education to the teaching associated with them stems from the fact that the compilers of the Agreed Syllabuses used the calendar of the Church's year as the framework for R.E. in the primary school. (The traditional sandwiching of the life and teaching of Jesus between these two festivals has caused more than one young child to express astonishment that Jesus could have grown up and died so quickly!)

In the secondary school syllabuses Christmas and Easter were treated less as festivals; rather they came into courses on the 'Life of Christ'. Even a course based on Mark's Gospel would have the nativity stories from Matthew and Luke added.

The very familiarity of all that is associated with Christmas and Easter makes it difficult to take a really objective look at how they are being handled, but unless we do this quite rigorously we shall find that they stand out in startling contrast to the rest of what we are doing in religious education.

There is one sense in which they already help to achieve one of our aims in R.E.—they illustrate the relationship between religion and culture. It is not only practising Christians who celebrate Christmas or who buy Easter eggs and take advantage of the Easter holidays. At First school level this will be implicit in the fact that everyone shares in the activities. At Middle school level it will become more explicit as the children find out, for example, that customs associated with the festivals acquire their own particular form in different countries. For senior pupils it will be an important part of the study of a religion as a whole, but it can also come in incidentally. A class of (non-academic) 13 year olds who had recently learned the rules of formal debating tackled with great seriousness, and with no intervention from the teacher, the motion, 'This house believes that only Christians should celebrate Christmas'.

However, we must be sure that, as well as serving this aim, our handling of Christmas and Easter will also contribute positively to the pupils' understanding of Christianity. This applies of course to every part of the syllabus; the presentation of one aspect of a religion must always be true to the religion as a whole.

The irony is that it is within traditional R.E., with its concern for passing on the Christian faith to the pupils, that the approach to Christmas and Easter is so much at variance with what the Christian faith really stands for.

If we analyse this rather startling accusation we find that the problems relate both to the Christian Scriptures and to Christian theology.

Part of our aim in religious education is that our pupils should learn how to handle the Christian Scriptures properly. This is a gradual process and the steps in it will be discussed later (see pp.82 ff.), but we shall obviously not want to use biblical material in any way that would impede this process. How then might it be impeded by what we do at Christmas and Easter?

It has been customary in the primary school to tell 'the story' from the Bible in the period preceding the festival. This tends to happen each year—even though in no other aspect of the curriculum do children encounter this kind of repetition. Quite apart from the fact that such a practice produces the idea that the stories are really for small children, serious questions are raised by the conflation of the material in the different Gospels. There is no such thing as 'the' Bible story about the birth of Jesus. There are two Bible stories, and the one in Matthew is different in many respects from the one in Luke.

When we come to Easter we find four accounts, one in each of the Gospels. The Christmas 'story' is made up by weaving together the two accounts. The Easter 'story' is made up by selecting elements from some or all of the four accounts. It is not possible to make a continuous narrative by using all of the Easter stories because the accounts are actually mutually exclusive. For example, in the first three Gospels the crucifixion takes place after the Passover meal, in John before it; in Matthew Jesus' first resurrection appearance to his disciples is in Galilee, in Luke and John it is in Jerusalem.

It would be quite wrong to try to explain away the variations by likening them to the differences to be found in eye-witnesses' accounts of an incident. The situation is completely different (see p.104). It may well be that some details got altered as the stories were handed on, but there is very much more to it than that. Each of the Gospel writers had certain themes which he wanted to emphasise and he often selected his material in order to illustrate these themes. Luke traces the genealogy of Jesus back to Adam, in keeping with the universalistic emphasis of his Gospel, Matthew traces it back to Abraham, in keeping with his Jewish emphasis. Luke, with his concern for the outcast, emphasises the lowliness of Jesus' birth. Matthew on the other hand makes no mention of the stable or 'no room at the inn' or the good news being proclaimed to one of the despised occupations—shepherds. Much in Matthew's Gospel as a whole seems to have been designed to show Jesus as a second Moses and it is not surprising, therefore, to find that the introduction to the Gospel contains stories of Jesus' birth which are reminiscent of those surrounding the birth of Moses—the rescue of the baby from the massacre of the male children and the sojourn in Egypt. There is no need to multiply examples. A careful reading of the Gospels will show the differences in the accounts and a good commentary will discuss the reasons for them.

What are the implications of all this for religious education?

With the youngest children the conflation of the two Christmas stories is perhaps less serious, but on the other hand we should be concentrating on using the ideas and the imagery from the stories rather than on 'telling' the stories. For reasons that we shall come to, the Easter stories will probably not figure at all during the First school years.

When the children can read fairly easily they should be encouraged to find out which parts of 'the story' are in Luke and which in Matthew. It is only adults who are likely to be upset by this approach to the hallowed tradition; children fall on the task with enthusiasm. The recognition that there are two stories will be extended through other units of study in the Middle school years, e.g., with the reminder from the teacher as the class check the story of the Wise Men that it is only in Matthew's Gospel. This kind of incidental reinforcement is as important as actual units of study, but to be able to make the most effective use of it the teacher has to be thoroughly familiar with the whole pattern of religious education and the areas in which understanding must be gradually built up.

The biblical material about Easter will play a less prominent part in the Middle school years than the Christmas material, but the same principle applies. We should never make up our own Easter 'story' by putting together incidents drawn from different Gospels—or use versions in which this has already been done for us, because whatever the original sequence of events might have been, it certainly will not be the sequence we have concocted.

For older pupils the work on the Christian Scriptures associated with the unit 'Sacred Writings' gives scope for a really scholarly look at the nativity stories, and the Easter stories will come into the unit 'Who was Jesus?'. (The word 'scholarly' must not be misunderstood. It does not mean that only academically able pupils can look at the nativity stories in this way. The approach will need to be completely different for less able pupils and the study less ambitious in extent, but the same aims apply. See pp.18 f., 131 ff.) The success of such study at this level will be greatly affected by the understanding (or misunderstanding) which the pupils bring with them from their earlier encounter with the stories.

We now turn to the ways in which the traditional teaching about Christmas and Easter is at variance with the Christian faith.

In Christian theology Christmas and Easter are associated particularly with the doctrines of the Incarnation and Salvation. The material in the Gospels is one way of expressing that theology, but it can be seen as such only when it is fully understood and set in the context of the biblical teaching as a whole. The stories themselves do not necessarily convey the theology, and certainly not to children.

Let us take Christmas first. To Christians the doctrine of the Incarnation speaks of God's involvement in this world and of the consequent destroying of the barriers between the sacred (God's world) and the secular (not God's world). It speaks of the nature of God as personal, revealed in a human life—a *real* human life? It speaks of the humility of God, shown in Jesus' lowly birth—the helpless babe at Bethlehem. And it speaks of the universality of God's love—God became man for the sake of all men.

We can check how much of all this children are likely to understand from the Christmas stories—and from the traditional nativity play. The universality of God's love will probably have been grasped, from the message of goodwill given to the shepherds and from the story of the Wise Men. The barrier between the sacred and the secular, however, will have been reinforced by the fact that Jesus apparently came from 'God's world' into 'our world'. The supernatural accompaniment—messages from God delivered by angels and an archangel, a miraculous star, and a heavenly choir in the sky—make it difficult if not impossible for children to think of Jesus as fully human or to grasp the real significance of the lowliness of his birth.

The traditional form of the nativity play only underlines this. The very characteristics which endear it to the heart of the 'mums' are those that remove it most effectively from the events it seeks to portray. The hygienic scene, in which everything looks 'lovely', is a far cry from the sordid circumstances in which a young girl had to give birth to her first child. The Christian doctrine of the Incarnation is certainly not reflected in the conventional tableau.

The relationship between the beliefs of a religion and its scriptures will form part of the study of older pupils, and one of the discoveries they will make is that in no religion can one just 'read off' the beliefs from those parts of the scriptures which are in narrative form. Stories have an important function in religion, but they are not to be confused with theology, which is a systematic statement of beliefs.

What then do we do about Christmas in the nine or ten years of religious education that precede this kind of study? It is certainly not being suggested that the stories should be banned. They are a very rich part of the child's heritage. But we should concentrate more on *using* them and less on just *telling* them (and we should certainly avoid repeating them in much the same form each year).

This kind of suggestion usually evokes the protest, 'But the children must know the Bible story'. What is this story? Quite apart from the fact that, as we have seen, there are two separate stories in the Gospels, once we include the three kings we have moved right away from the biblical version, which merely refers to the visitors as 'wise men from the East'. What a lot we should lose if we omitted those three picturesque monarchs!

For the youngest children it is the imagery of the stories that is most important. It is of the nature of imagery that it communicates at a deeper level than mere intellectual understanding and it does not depend for its effect on knowing the exact form of the story. One class of five year olds made a large Christmas collage. There were 27 woolly sheep on a hillside becuase there were 27 children in school the day they made the sheep. There were 29 kings, in splendid cloaks made from gay scraps of material. How much poorer would the experience of those children have been if their teacher had insisted on 'getting the story right'. A small village school (a Church school) made an enormous mural to which every child in the school contributed. It was a joyous riot of colour in which angels and stars, Christmas trees and Santa Claus, the twelve days of Christmas, the stable, the shepherds and the kings all found a place. And rightly so, for that was what Christmas meant to those children.

For pupils of about eight to twelve there are units which help them to think about the significance of the Christmas imagery (see pp.168–9). And when they explore the truths which Christians wanted to express through the legendary additions to the biblical story of the Wise Men, they are on the way to understanding that even within the Bible there are stories which express significant truths even though they are not actually historical. This is an important preparation for the kind of study of the Bible, and particularly of the Nativity stories, which older pupils will be undertaking.

The Christmas stories (or parts of them) can also serve as starting points for themes on a variety of subjects. A theme on 'Babies' for the fives to sixes at Christmas time does not need to be prefaced by the telling of the stories; all that is necessary is a reference to the birth of the baby Jesus at Christmas. A reference to 'no room at the inn' makes an introduction to a study of homelessness at the Junior stage.

It is helpful at Christmas time to tackle themes and read stories which in some way explore the areas of human experience spoken about in the Christian doctrine of the Incarnation—giving, sharing, the value of the whole of life, the significance of *every* man, concern for those whom society does not consider important, etc.—so that children come to associate these values with Christmas even though there is no reference to Christian theology. It will be a much more useful preparation for the study in the Upper school of such questions as 'What do Christians mean by the Incarnation?' than just knowing the Christmas stories.

If Christmas has its difficulties they pale into insignificance beside those associated with Easter.

We have already referred to the four Easter 'stories', but that is a misleading term because accounts of the Passion—the events leading up to the death of Jesus—and of the Resurrection take up between a quarter and a third of each of the Gospels. We are therefore dealing with a considerable amount of material and not with brief self-contained stories.

The Easter events are the focal point of the Christian doctrine of Salvation. This doctrine speaks to Christians of God's initiative in saving man, of the conquest of evil by self-giving love, of reconciliation, and of the offer to man of a new quality of life.

If we check this as we did with the doctrine of the Incarnation and ask how much of it children are likely to have understood from the Easter stories, the result is indeed negative. To children God can appear cruel because he let Jesus die. The most deep-seated concept of God held by children (and often by adults as well) is his power. God is 'almighty', God can do anything. And if the children have had 'evidence' of this in miracle stories and stories about God intervening to look after Moses and David and Elijah and Daniel, then the fact that he didn't save Jesus from death is disturbing. If God was so obviously involved in the events surrounding the birth of Jesus, and if Jesus was the Son of God, then why did God abandon him when he most needed help? And the words that Mark and Matthew record as spoken by Jesus on the cross— 'My God, my God, why hast thou forsaken me?' only serve to underline that question. The death of Jesus will appear to many children not as God's act of salvation but as a sad defeat of Jesus by wicked men.

The problem does not lie in the violence of the story as is sometimes suggested. Children can take violence in their stride. But they have a strong sense of justice which is satisfied only when the 'goodies' win and the 'baddies' are defeated. Children identify with the 'goodies' in a story and if the 'baddies' are killed they feel nothing but a sense of reassurance that the world really is all right. If a 'goody' suffers or is killed the reaction is completely different, and it is in the light of this fact that we must see the account of the death of Jesus.

The advice frequently offered to teachers is to put the emphasis on the Resurrection, but this 'solution' misses the mark on two counts. In the first place it gives an impression that is false to Christian theology— implying that God somehow waved a wand and made everything come right again. The reality of the cross for Christians—the conquest of evil by self-giving love, gives way to the popular concept of God's power.

Secondly, we have to ask what children understand by the expression 'came to life again'. The small girl who asked, 'How could he be alive if he's dead?' expressed the puzzlement of many. Children interpret in the context of their experience, and in their experience death is final. When relatives or pets have died they don't reappear. And where children have been told about life after death it is certainly not in the form of coming back to this life.

There is another important consideration. That Jesus was crucified is a historical fact. That God raised him from the dead is a theological affirmation. It is a belief held only by Christians. We cannot therefore teach it in school as if it was universally accepted. It comes into the category of statement that must be prefaced by 'Christians believe'. What Christians believe about the resurrection of Jesus and the impact of that belief will form part of the study of older pupils; it only raises insuperable problems if we try to deal with it too early.

If the traditional telling of the Easter stories is so fraught with problems, what can we do instead?

As with Christmas we can create an association of ideas with the Easter season without running into the dangers described above. There are two main emphases—new life, and coming to terms with the dark side.

Spring, or some aspect of it, is an excellent theme for the Easter season (a combination unfortunately denied to teachers in the southern hemisphere!). Spring is already celebrated annually in some form or another in most First school classes. Planting dry brown bulbs and watching for the first signs of life and then the growth towards full flowering, seeing the gradual unfurling of leaf buds on trees and bushes, etc., is to experience once again the miracle of new life returning to the earth. And if the children are able to watch chickens hatching they will have the added experience of witnessing not only the miracle of new life but also the effort and struggle demanded from the chick—literally a life and death struggle—and this awareness is a most important counter to too sentimental an approach to spring.

'Night and Day' or 'Light and Darkness' are appropriate themes for slightly older children to explore in the second half of the spring term. They provide a way of marking the arrival of the new season without having to repeat the 'Spring' theme through the Junior school years, and they make it possible to broaden the study to include ideas and material suited to the stage of the children's development.

For the Middle school years there will be references to Easter in the unit 'Signs and Symbols'—Easter eggs, baby rabbits and chickens, hot cross buns, etc., as well as the cross itself. And Easter will obviously play a larger part in the unit 'Festivals'.

As has already been suggested (see pp.42 ff.) the use of literature is one of the best means of helping children in the First and Middle School years to come to terms with the dark side of life. In addition to this, biographies provide for Middle school pupils an appropriate way of exploring those areas of experience associated with Easter—people who brought new life to others (e.g., Mario Borrelli), people who were prepared to sacrifice their own lives for the sake of others (e.g., Father Damien), or people whose spirit triumphed over darkness and suffering (e.g., Anne Frank).

For senior pupils the unit 'Who was Jesus?' will involve discovering what is meant by 'the Easter faith', and a study of the significance for Christians of the Cross and the Resurrection will be part of the units 'Suffering' and 'Life after Death'. It is really only at this stage in adolescence that it is possible to understand without distortion the place of Easter in the Christian faith. Those teachers of younger children who are anxious about giving up their annual telling of the Easter stories or the making of a model of the Easter garden will perhaps be less reluctant when they see their section of the religious education syllabus in the light of the whole, and realise that a different approach will in the long run achieve a much more positive understanding of the Christian festivals.

12

Sacred writings

Sacred literature is one of the important phenomena of religion and it will therefore constitute a major element in religious education, serving not only to introduce pupils to some of the teachings of the main religions but also to illustrate the role that sacred writings play within religions.

The word 'writings' obscures the fact that in most religions there was a period—in some of them a very long period—during which the traditions were passed on in oral and not in written form. It also obscures the fact that primal religions do not have a canon of scripture, i.e., a fixed body of traditions regarded as especially authoritative and committed to writing. However, as long as these two facts are recognised and form part of the pupils' study, it is convenient to use the expression 'sacred writings'. This expression has been chosen rather than 'scriptures' because there are some writings which have great influence in a religion even though they are technically not scriptures.

A fairly substantial unit on 'Sacred Writings' is suggested for the 13–15 age group (see pp.157–8), but this should certainly not be the first time that pupils encounter the subject. In some ways it is one of the topics for which we need the most careful preparation in the earlier years. Sacred writings in any religion were written for adults and not for children. They contain many of the beliefs of a religion but these beliefs can seldom be 'read off' in any simple fashion. Scriptures are interpreted writings. They belong to a community, they 'live' within that community, and they are interpreted within the total faith of that community. An example of this is the body of literature which constitutes both the Jewish Bible and the Christian Old Testament—the words are identical but there are many variations in the way in which the two communities interpret them.

In this country where, because of our cultural heritage, Christianity is the religion that pupils will be studying at greatest depth, it is the

Bible which they will encounter first at school and meet most frequently in the Middle and Upper school years. However, this is certainly not the mixture as before. A completely different approach from that which characterised traditional R.E. will be necessary. The declared aim of the compilers of the Agreed Syllabuses was to communicate the Christian faith. If our aim now is to help pupils to understand what religion is, then our handling of the Christian Scriptures must be in line both with that overall aim and with the sectional aim of helping them to understand the role of sacred writings within religions.

When scriptures are used within a community of faith they are one of the ways in which the community says: 'This is what God is like' or 'This is the way things are'. When they are used outside the community of faith their status changes. They now become examples of how Christians—or Jews or Hindus—understand reality or (and this is a very important distinction for some religions) how they understood it at a particular period in their history. Because the school is not part of a community of faith, even where its teachers and many of its pupils happen to be members of a particular religious community, it cannot use the scriptures of any religion to say to the pupils 'This is the way things are' or 'This is what God is like'. There will of course be some material in any scriptures which, because of its insight into the human situation, evokes a response from readers outside the community of faith and makes them want to say, 'Yes, this *is* the way things are', but the beliefs that make a religion distinctive must be presented in school as the beliefs of that religion and not as absolute truth.

One of the ways in which we can help pupils to develop an understanding of the nature of the Christian Scriptures is to identify any biblical material we use. For example, any Old Testament stories we tell to the under nines should be put into the context of 'stories Jesus heard as a boy'. This is factually accurate and it serves to build up in the child's mind the idea of a category of stories which were there before Jesus' time and were important to someone growing up within Judaism. This is an early stage in the process of recognising the Jewish Scriptures.

In the Middle school years it is possible to identify material more precisely. At this stage children are only beginning to develop a sense of history so we shall not expect them to be able to fit Old Testament material into any historical sequence, but they can recognise the difference between 'in the very early days when they were nomads' for the Patriarchal narratives about Abraham, Isaac and Jacob, or 'when the people of Israel had a land of their own' for stories after the entry into Canaan.

This of course presumes that the teachers have acquired the necessary knowledge themselves. The practice of just finding a book of Bible stories and reading one to the class is absolutely out. Even checking the story in the Bible is not enough. Teachers must know the nature of the material they are handling. Teaching R.E. requires as much rigorous preparation as other subjects in the curriculum—if not more.

A more systematic attempt to distinguish different kinds of literature in the Old Testament would be undertaken in the unit 'Synagogue School at the Time of Jesus' in the Junior school years. Here the children would find out that in the Jewish Bible there were types of writing similar to those they were familiar with—poetry, history, stories, laws, etc.—and that these were written at different times and for different purposes. They would also learn something about Hebrew. Children adore copying out Hebrew words and short passages and putting the English translation underneath. They also enjoy 'playing' with the Hebrew alphabet, and in the process of trying to put their own names into Hebrew they discover (and will remember) that there are no vowels in the alphabet. Copying out a passage in English, but following the Hebrew style of the biblical period, i.e., no vowels, no capitals, no spaces between the words and no punctuation, is fun (and why shouldn't religious education be fun?). It also produces a respect for the difficulties which boys in the synagogue school had to cope with, and it is laying the foundation for a later understanding of the task of translators and other scholars who work on the biblical text.

The synagogue school unit could be followed in the Middle school years by a study of two or three of the books of the Bible (including this time the New Testament). The purpose would not be to teach the children the contents or the 'message' of the books, though they would certainly learn something of the content in the course of their study, but rather to encourage them to do some detective work on the writings, to discover what can be known of their origin, authorship, destination and purpose. It is in other words a methodological study, enabling the pupils to gain some insight into the work that biblical scholars do. Only a few of the books are suitable for this age group, but possible ones are Daniel, Mark and Philemon and, for the twelves to thirteens, Jonah and 1 Corinthians and possibly Acts.

A great deal of misunderstanding of the biblical material will be avoided if we concentrate on helping pupils to handle the material properly before attempting any systematic teaching of its content.

Units on life in Bible times and on biblical archaeology will also make their contribution to the pupils' growing understanding of the kind of book—or rather collection of books—that the Bible is. And so will the kind of approach that is suggested for teaching about Jesus—perhaps the most difficult of all the biblical material to handle well. The use of the Christmas and Easter stories has already been discussed (see pp.73 f.). The use of other material about Jesus will be dealt with in chapter 14.

Most of the units suggested for the thirteen-plus age groups will make some reference to biblical material. If this study is to be of real value it is obvious that the pupils must know the principles involved in 'using' the Bible. Otherwise they just assume that everything in it is to be taken at face value and all passages treated in an identical manner. Such literalism tends to produce a minority who adopt a rigid doctrinaire approach—'the Bible says . . .' and therefore it must be so—and a majority whose scepticism about some aspects leads them to an equally rigid uncritical rejection of the lot. Both these positions make any serious study of the Bible impossible.

We have shown how a gradual understanding of the Christian Scriptures will be built up during the years of a pupil's schooling. However, he should also have met the sacred writings of other religions before undertaking the unit 'Sacred Writings'.

The way in which scriptures are used, especially in worship, and the reverence with which they are treated, will be met in the unit 'Sacred Places'. This knowledge will be extended and the pupils will also learn about some of the content in the unit 'Festivals'.

The unit 'Sacred Writings' includes a fairly substantial study of the scriptures and of other writings which are regarded as authoritative within the major religions, so that pupils will be aware of the quite different types of literature, the different ways in which they came into being, and the different role which each has within its own religion. This will provide a foundation on which later study can be built. For instance, it will be necessary for the study of individual religions, and it will make a contribution to the unit 'Worship'. And in the units 'What is Man?', 'Suffering' and 'Life after Death' it is absolutely essential for the pupils to be able to assess the status of the literature from which they are drawing ideas. Their conclusions will be completely misleading if they are not able to distinguish between, e.g., poetry and court chronicles, or early material and later editings.

A different kind of problem faces us when we look in other religions for the equivalent of Bible stories. The Judaeo-Christian Scriptures are unique in containing so many passages in dramatic narrative form. There are no such stories in the Hindu Vedas and Upanishads, in the Buddhist Pali Canon, in the Sikh Granth or in the Muslim Qur'an.

There *are* examples of teaching in vivid parable form. For example, in the Chandogya Upanishad (VI, 13) there is the famous illustration of the man who told his son to put a piece of salt in water and the next morning asked him to bring the salt back to him. When the son couldn't find the salt his father told him to taste the water, from the sides and from the middle. The salt taste was everywhere the same in the water but the salt could not be seen. This is similar in some ways to the New Testament parables. The details of the story are easy to understand but the truth it is pointing to is profound. Six year olds could follow the story of the salt at one level but they could certainly not grasp its teaching about the relationship of *Atman*, the spirit of man, with *Brahman*, the spirit of the universe.

If a story is a satisfying story in itself, and if it does not make it difficult for children later on to grasp its religious meaning, then it can be included in the teacher's repertoire. The age of the children makes all the difference here. The story of the salt may be right for the young Hindu child growing up within the community of faith, because it is one of the beliefs of that community which is expressed through the story. But for other children of First school age it has nothing in common with the stories we would normally choose to tell them, and they certainly would understand nothing of its real meaning. The story could have a place though in the Middle school years, because not only does its form make an appeal at this age, but it raises the question of continuity and change, sameness and difference, which is a fundamental aspect of human experience. So although one would not be trying to explain the complex beliefs of Hinduism about the nature of reality to nines to thirteens the story would be a useful preparation both for meeting that belief later and also for the more systematic consideration of what it is to be human in units like 'Who am I?' and 'What is Man?'

Although the scriptures of other faiths do not provide us with many stories for children, there is in each of the religions a certain amount of traditional literature which can be used. In Hinduism the two great epics, the Ramayana and the Mahabharata, are technically not scriptures, but they are much more popular with the ordinary Hindu than the Vedas and the Upanishads, and they certainly come into the category of 'sacred writings'. There are many stories of Rama and Sita which have been retold for children. One version can be found in *Indian Tales and Legends* by J. E. B. Gray. B. L. Picard has retold the story of the Mahabharata under the title *The Story of the Pandavas*. This is beautifully written and suitable for nines to thirteens, but because of the large number of characters and the great complexity of the plot it is better for individual reading than for general use in class.

Where there are children of other faiths in a school, very serious consideration must be given to including stories which are part of their cultural heritage. This not only has the psychological effect of reassuring the children that they are accepted (for to ignore a child's culture is tantamount to rejecting the child himself), but it also adds richness and breadth to the experience of the rest of the class.

However, handling stories from other people's religions has just as many pitfalls for the unwary as handling biblical stories. One teacher enthusiastically made a collection of Indian tales only to discover that they were regarded by the Indians themselves as inferior examples of their literature.

Publishers are increasingly becoming aware of the need to make available the traditional literature of other cultures, particularly those represented in Britain, but quality varies widely and it is wise to seek advice as to what is really worth using, either from the education departments of the religions or from the advisory service for teachers of the Christian Education Movement or the Shap Working Party (see p.178 for addresses).

We have already discussed in general terms the sensitivity needed for handling other men's faiths (see chapters 8 and 9) but there are several points which relate particularly to sacred writings.

Let us look first at the use of stories. What do we do about the miraculous element? It would obviously not be right to dismiss as fiction the accounts of gods appearing to men, or vessels which filled up again as soon as they were emptied, in the stories of Hinduism, while at the same time treating as historical biblical stories of God and angels appearing to men, or the widow's cruse of oil that never ran dry. Nor would it be right to adopt a completely sceptical approach to the miraculous element in all sacred writings.

Some of our difficulties become less acute if we are able to present the material in the context of 'stories people liked to tell', but the most important consideration is the approach that the religious communities themselves adopt. If we cannot reconcile that approach with the needs of our pupils then the material is obviously not suitable for use with children of that age and must be postponed until the pupils are old enough to understand its function within the religion.

Sometimes teachers are advised to use stories from religious literature in exactly the same way that they use other stories, for example, telling the 'myths and legends' of the Bible just as they would tell the myths and legends of Greece. But the issue isn't as simple as it might appear. The God who figures in the biblical stories is the God whom Jews and Christians worship today, but the stories come out of an early stage in the development of these religions. God is sometimes pictured as acting in ways which no longer express adequately what men believe about him. For example, in the Exodus stories God not only rescues his own people—Moses and the Israelites—but he brings about the death of thousands of Egyptians in the process. The events of the Exodus were part of the process by which Israel came to understand that God was a saving God, and in the Upper school stage this will be an important part of the pupils' study (for instance, in the unit 'Pilgrim People'), but it is impossible for First school children to distinguish between the 'God' in these stories and the 'God' whom Jews and Christians worship today.

This problem is not so acute in the Middle school years because by then children are able to understand that men believed something at one stage in their history and that later they thought about it differently. However, it is essential to explain this when introducing such material; pupils are not likely to make the distinction otherwise.

The cycle of stories about Jacob also serves to illustrate a problem which we might encounter in the literature of any living religion. Children's strong sense of justice is offended by the fact that God blesses Jacob. They ask why God not only let Jacob get away with all those acts of selfishness and deceit, but actually approved them by giving Jacob his blessing.

Although the aim of religious education is not confessional, teaching for belief, we must be just as concerned with the religious concepts that children develop as if it were. We have to be scrupulously fair to the beliefs of all faiths, and it is certainly not the function of R.E. to do anything that would make it more difficult for the pupils to understand what the members of living religions believe.

Doing justice to religions also involves being very careful about comparisons. One R.E. scheme of work on 'Rules' for the Middle school presented the Golden Rule (Lk. 6:31; Mt. 7:12) for Christianity, but chose the Ten Commandments for Judaism. This completely ignores the famous story about Hillel, one of the great Jewish Rabbis who died when Jesus was about 15. When a man asked Hillel to teach him the whole of the Jewish Law while standing on one leg, the Rabbi answered, 'What is hateful to you, do not do to your neighbour. This is the whole Law, the rest is commentary on it. Go and learn.' The Golden Rule has been developed in several religions, and this is a significant fact which should be discussed, not ignored.

The teacher who directs the attention of pupils to extracts from the sacred writings of different religions has to walk a kind of tight-rope. On the one hand, as we have just seen, he must allow similar teachings to be recognised. There are many of these—dealing with concern for the needy, self-forgetfulness, self-control, the uselessness of words not matched by deeds, the importance of sincerity, etc. On the other hand he must not follow the example of the teacher who selected only similar teachings in an attempt to convince his pupils that there was nothing to choose between religions. There are similar teachings and there are distinctive teachings and any serious—and honest—study of sacred writings must include both.

Another important point to be born in mind—and to be understood by the pupils, is that one cannot just make straightforward comparisons between the sacred writings of one religion and those of another. One first has to ask what is the nature of the writing being considered. Poems or narrative accounts cannot be put alongside accounts of direct teaching as if there were no difference between them. The form of the literature obviously affects the way its language is to be interpreted.

One also has to ask what is the role of the literature within its community of faith, and therefore its authority for the members of that community. It would, for example, be wrong to treat the Muslim Qur'an as if it were the same as the Christian Bible. The place of the

Qur'an in Islam is more like the place of Christ in Christianity. To Muslims the Qur'an is the Word of God—its words are God's words, not Muhammad's. For Muslims all the words of the Qur'an still carry complete authority. By contrast, most Christians would regard sections of the Bible as descriptive accounts of the early stages of their religion. Not many, for example, consider themselves bound by the laws in the Book of Leviticus or even by some of the commands recorded in the New Testament, e.g., that a woman should not pray without her head covered (I Cor. 11:5) or that all governments should be obeyed because they are ordained by God (Rom. 13:1).

Finally, one has to know how far one can generalise from teachings to be found in sacred writings. Hindu literature provides perhaps the most vivid example of the dangers of generalising. The Vedas, the Upanishads and the Bhagavad-Gita contain very different emphases. The Gods—associated with nature—figure in the Vedas; the Upanishads are mainly monistic, i.e., there is one underlying Spirit in the universe, within which everything belongs; while the Gita emphasises devotion to the God Krishna. These differences are not only developments in the course of time; all these strands can be found in Hinduism today. So one can neither select just one strand, nor try to amalgamate them, and say 'This is what Hindus believe'.

In addition to this, sacred writings are often interpreted differently by different groups within religious communities. The spectrum of biblical interpretation we are familiar with is by no means unique to Christianity, and we must not fall into the trap of implying that there is only one approach to the sacred writings of other religions just because we don't encounter the variety, the controversy and the questioning in the way that we encounter them in relation to the Christian Bible.

It is mainly because neither teachers nor pupils can be expected to have any detailed knowledge of the complexity of the sacred writings of other religions and their place within their own cultural and religious tradition that, in this country, it is the Christian Scriptures which will be used most frequently to illustrate the nature and the use of sacred writings.

13

... The Bible

We have already had reason to make a number of references to the Christian Scriptures (see chapters 9, 11 and 12). There are, however, several points which need to be considered in a more systematic way if the Bible is to be used as the main illustration of sacred writings.

Religion and culture are inextricably interwoven. It is stating the obvious to say that all sacred writings came out of a particular culture and were written at a particular time. The implications of this for the use of the Bible in religious education, however, have not always been so obvious. For instance, the Agreed Syllabuses seemed to assume that there was no cultural barrier to children's understanding of the biblical stories.

What are the main problems?

The Bible is a collection of writings that came into being over a period of a thousand years—between 2,000 and 3,000 years ago—and it covers a period of history which goes back almost 1,000 years earlier still. The events it describes and the life it portrays are those of a group of countries in the Middle East. Many of the background details which would be needed if this material from an alien culture was to make sense to children growing up in an Anglo-saxon culture in the twentieth century are not included in the text. The original readers did not need them because they were the shared experience of the writers and their readers. The material in the Bible was written for immediate use. It was addressed to, and meant to be applied in, the contemporary situation. It was never intended by its authors to be bound in black covers and 'studied' two to three thousand years later.

Without the relevant background knowledge some passages can be completely misunderstood, and many yield a much more superficial meaning than they would have done to their original readers.

Take, for example, the parable of the Good Samaritan (Lk. 10). To most children it appears to be a simple story about someone in need and two 'nasty' men who passed by and one 'nice' man who helped. How much more profound it becomes when one knows the history of the relationships between the Samaritans and the Jews, the nature of the terrain of the road from Jerusalem to Jericho, the fact that pilgrims on their way to Jerusalem from the north used this long difficult route to avoid going through Samaria, the meaning of the technical term 'neighbour', the fact that priests and Levites had periods of duty in the Temple in Jerusalem and that contact with a dead body could make it impossible for them to carry out their duties.

Even these brief references, which could be expanded considerably, show that where the background is not known there is a tendency to trivialise the story.

This of course raises the question of whether we should tell biblical stories to children before they are old enough to understand the background. It is often argued that young children should have the story at the 'simple' level they can cope with and then later they can learn its deeper meaning, but there is plenty of evidence to show that the repetition of stories through the primary school can eventually make pupils resistant to them by the time they reach the stage when they could understand their real significance.

A small number of biblical stories will come into religious education during the Junior school years, and when we do tell them it is important that we should put in the background details that are needed to bring them to life. However, more important at this stage is learning about life in Bible times.

This is the stage when children have a tremendous curiosity. They love to amass factual information. They become experts on prehistoric animals, aeroplanes, the Romans, the Vikings—but how seldom are they allowed to satisfy their longing for 'real' information in religious education. They need lots of detail. When they are interested in anything they like to find out all about it. This is one of the reasons why teachers have sometimes found background schemes unsuccessful. Children are likely to be bored where the information is slight or superficial, as it is in so many books on life in Bible times written for use in schools.

One of the dangers of any study of a way of life from the distant past is the tendency to turn it into a comparison with life now. Children may well react negatively to a way of life that lacked TV, cars, telephone, etc. There are three ways to counteract this tendency.

First, the children should be helped to see Palestinian life in the context of the way of life of some other people in the distant past, for example, the Romans or the ancient Britons. Secondly, the emphasis should be put not on comparisons with life now but on discovering about life then. Thirdly, the children's attention should be directed not only to externals, to the amenities of life, but to values (e.g., the close-knit family relationship in Judaism, or the strict laws of hospitality among nomadic peoples) and to factors which call forth respect and admiration (e.g., the fact that most Jewish people in Palestine would have to know three languages, or the toughness of the life of the fisher-man or shepherd).

How do we decide which aspects of life in Bible times to include? The first consideration is the age of the pupils. For six to eight year olds it would be centred mainly on home life. Nine to twelve year olds would be able to extend the area of their study. But in either case we should be influenced in our selection by what helps the children to enter imaginatively and sympathetically into the life of the people being studied. A scheme on life in Palestine at the time of Jesus which concen-trated on houses, clothes and food would have done little to enable the children to enter into the life of a Jewish family, for it would have left out those things which characterised Jewish family life—the close relationship between a boy and his father, the stories from the Scriptures, the Synagogue school, the visit to the Synagogue on the Sabbath, the journey to the Temple at Jerusalem at Passover time, etc.

This kind of study, if handled properly, makes an important contri-bution to R.E. in three ways. It develops a positive attitude to Judaism, which is part of our aim of helping pupils to understand the major religions. It is an essential foundation for later study of the origins of Christianity, because Jesus was a Jew and many Jewish beliefs and values are part of the heritage of Christianity. And it provides the kind of background knowledge which makes possible an understanding of the content of much of the material in the New Testament.

The biblical image theme is another form which background study can take. There are a number of images in the Bible which have entered into our way of thinking and speaking and which are frequently met in English literature. The most significant images, in the order in which they should be tackled in R.E., are Shepherd, Bread, Water, Light, Fire, Pilgrim People.

A people's images emerge out of its way of life, and a real understanding of the significance of an image can therefore be gained only by learning about the way of life that produced it. It is only when one knows about the life of the nomadic shepherd, who would spend days or even weeks alone with his flock, leading them across barren hills to find pasture and water, and whom they would follow with complete trust, that one can start to understand why the image of the good shepherd came to denote a close relationship of care and trust.

With the under tens it is probably sufficient to learn about the life of the shepherd, but from about ten pupils should be able to discuss the fact of the image, and compare it with images which have emerged out of our way of life, e.g., images related to the sea or royalty or sport, reflected in numerous expressions in our language ('when the tide turns', 'treated royally', 'it isn't cricket').

Senior pupils would quite consciously set out to discover, in the theme 'Pilgrim People', what it was in the experience of the people of Israel and of the early Church that made the image of always being on a journey so evocative. In the process of making this discovery they would actually be doing a historical study. However, instead of the traditional working through the history of Israel and of the early Church over a period of a year or two, they would focus on those aspects—early nomadic period, the Exodus, the nature of the monarchy, the challenge of the prophets, the Exile, etc.—which explain the emergence of the image. It is perhaps worth mentioning that this kind of study actually includes most of what pupils in general R.E. (as opposed to those doing R.S. for examination purposes) need to know of the history of Israel. It is tackling a historical study at the stage when pupils have developed the capacity to handle historical development and it brings together and puts into historical sequence many of the things which the pupils will have met in their earlier studies.

Another topic which serves a number of useful purposes in religious education is biblical archaeology. This belongs mainly in the Middle school years. Finding out what light archaeology throws on the biblical period is one way of increasing background knowledge. It also serves to anchor the story of the biblical peoples firmly in a historical and geographical setting. For too many pupils the biblical peoples seem to have a fictional quality, living their lives in a kind of vacuum. As pupils learn about Hammurabi's Code of Laws (dating from several hundred years before Moses), or about the remains of Phoenician temples which show what the plan of Solomon's Temple must have been like, they discover that in the biblical period, as in every other period in history, nations were in contact with each other, and that this response to encounter with other peoples is one of the main reasons for change and development within a religion.

Four biblical archaeology units are suggested on the chart. 'Masada' is the easiest to tackle, particularly for the non-specialist teacher, and it is probably the best one for the pupils to meet first. The boundaries of the topic are simpler to draw, the story of Yigael Yadin's archaeological expedition in 1963–64 is exciting and so is the story of the Zealots' last stand at Masada in A.D.73. It provides some insight not only into the intensity of the Zealots' attitude towards Rome but also into the spirit of modern Israel, symbolised in its determination that 'Masada shall not fall again!'.

There is yet another value in biblical archaeology units. It is useful for pupils to discover, before they reach the stage when they assume that science and religion are mutually exclusive, that the team of people engaged on any archaeological expedition includes specialists in a number of scientific disciplines.

Archaeology schemes should be used not only to discover what life was like at the time of the Patriarchs or in first century Palestine, but also to help pupils to learn how archaeologists work. The Middle school years are crucial for learning about learning, and we should be alert to opportunities of extending pupils' understanding of how men arrive at conclusions and what evidence they use and what factors they weigh in different areas of study.

The kind of religious education which we have been discussing will frequently take the pupils back to the Bible itself. The difference between this approach to the Bible and that of the Bible-centred syllabuses is first, that the use of the Bible will be much wider than it was when only stories were selected. Children learning about life in Bible times will look up all sorts of references which don't come into the passages considered suitable for children. (This is one reason why Children's Bibles or other shortened versions are no use. The *New English Bible* is the most reliable text. J. B. Phillips's translation and *Good News for Modern Man* are both readable versions.)

The second difference is that when the pupils do meet a biblical story their main concern will not be with its 'meaning' but with its illustration of life in Bible times. This is the right way round because, as we have seen, the content of any religion's sacred writings is intended for adults and it very often requires adult knowledge and adult experience to grasp the real meaning of a story.

This apparently random selection of biblical passages for background schemes is quite different from the random selection of stories for life-themes. In the latter case, not only is attention focussed on the meaning, with all the difficulties that raises for children, but it is a basically funda-mentalist use of the Bible. The stories are detached from their context, and no account is taken of the nature of the literature, the period when it was written, the purpose it originally served, or the way in which it is now interpreted in the religious community.

We have now moved from one aspect of sacred writings—their cultural context and the importance of knowing the cultural and religious back-ground—to another aspect—the different kinds of literature they contain, and the importance of being able to recognise these if the content is not to be misunderstood. The way in which the pupils' understanding of the literature of the Bible can be gradually built up was discussed in chapter 12, but one or two additional points need to be made here.

A method frequently advocated for helping pupils to realise that there are different kinds of writing in the Bible is to make a 'Bible library', perhaps with matchboxes, and write on the 'spine' of each 'book' History, Law, Prophecy, Letters, etc. However, this is so over-simplified that it is misleading. It may be quite safe to put Law on Leviticus and Prophecy on Isaiah and Jeremiah, but what about Daniel, which was not written in the prophetic period? (In the Jewish Bible Daniel is put with the Writings and not with the Prophets.) And what about Exodus, which includes history, law and poetry as well as chapters which describe the Tabernacle at a much later period? Or Genesis, where the first eleven chapters belong to a completely different category of literature from the patriarchal sagas of the rest of the book? The intention of the 'Bible library' is good, but discovering that there are different kinds of writing within books of the Bible is even more important, and it is better to build up that knowledge gradually in the way that has been outlined than try to do it through one particular activity.

Even more to be deplored is the practice of playing the 'Whispering game' in order to demonstrate how material in the Bible got changed in the process of being handed on. The analogy is a completely false one. Variations in the biblical text are not explained by someone's hearing not being sufficiently acute.

Some of the variations, like the Midianites and the Ishmaelites in Genesis 37 (who really rescued Joseph and took him into Egypt?), are there because the story became localised in two different regions of the country and when later editors wove the two versions into one story they left both heroes (Judah and Reuben) and both sets of foreign travellers.

Many factors were at work in the transmission of stories over a long period—factors familiar to students of oral transmission in any nation. But in addition to these normal processes, many of the writings were worked over by later editors. For example, eleven of the first twelve books of the Bible (i.e., excluding Ruth, which was written much later) were given their present form in the seventh to fifth centuries B.C. by editors who naturally put the earlier material into the context of what they *now* believed about God and his purpose for Israel. In the same way, the early Church was *using* the material which we have in the Gospels (see p.104). The Evangelists were not engaged in the mechanical task of trying to remember words and incidents—and they were certainly not whispering them to each other!

An interesting question is raised by our traditional practice of assuming that the New Testament starts where the Old Testament leaves off. In terms of history, the latest period dealt with in the O.T. is the fifth to fourth centuries B.C. (the time of Ezra and Nehemiah), and the last O.T. book to be written was probably Daniel (c.165 B.C.). This leaves an enormous gap before the first century A.D. New Testament.

Perhaps not surprisingly, many of the features of life and religion which the N.T. takes for granted are the results of developments during this inter-testamental period. The O.T. knows nothing of Sadducees, Pharisees, Zealots (or Essenes), synagogues, Rome's conquest of Palestine, Herod's rebuilding of the Temple, or belief in a devil, while belief in a resurrection makes only a brief appearance in two late O.T. writings. It was during this fascinating but neglected period that various things happened which explain many of the events and attitudes in the New Testament.

There was also the development of the Jewish Oral Tradition. Most Christians' 'knowledge' of this is confined to those passages in the

Gospels where it is dismissed as narrow legalism, and they are therefore unaware of its positive content or of the way in which the Rabbinic teachings developed gradually into the Talmud, that great repository of traditions which form the basis of Judaism today.

No study of the Judaeo-Christian sacred writings would be complete without recognising the developments both within the Jewish Bible (the way in which first the Law, then the Prophets and finally the Writings came to be regarded as 'scripture'), and beyond it into writings which have different degrees of authority in the religions. Most of this belongs in the thirteen-plus years, but Middle school pupils will have to go to 1 Maccabees in the Apocrypha when they are learning about the origin of Chanukah, the Jewish Feast of Lights, or when they are finding out about the Book of Daniel being written as a 'code book' during Antiochus Epiphanes' persecution. And in the First and Middle school years we must be careful to avoid any kind of teaching which is not consistent with these developments, such as assuming that Judaism is nothing more than what we find in the Old Testament and the pages of the New Testament.

We have now moved into the third main aspect of sacred writings which we must be concerned with in R.E.—their authority within the community of faith and the ways in which they are used within that community.

This will be illustrated most thoroughly in the unit 'Sacred Writings', and one of the most fruitful periods to study will be the period we have just been discussing—the second and first centuries B.C.E. and the first century C.E. ('Before the Common Era' and 'The Common Era'—used when referring to both Judaism and Christianity).

It is important, for example, for pupils to know that the first Christians took over the Jewish Bible as it stood, i.e., the Law and the Prophets, and later in the first century C.E. accepted the Jewish definition of what was to be included in the third section, the Writings. It is also important for them to know the different interpretation which Christians gave to sections of the Jewish Bible, particularly those passages which they interpreted as messianic.

Learning about the Septuagint (the translation of the Jewish Bible into Greek, often referred to as 'LXX') with its mixture of styles—some books translated literally word for word, others in a free and rather casual paraphrase—provides a useful corrective to the belief many pupils have that it was not until the biblical critics of the nineteenth century got to work that anyone had ever deviated from a faithful literalism. It is also important for pupils to discover that N.T. writers often use O.T. quotations to convey a different meaning from that of the original passage (cf. Isa. 40:3 and Mt. 3:3, and note the difference made by the punctuation of 'voice crying in the wilderness').

An understanding of the nature of the authority of its sacred writings for a religious community is essential before pupils use these writings for the units suggested for the Upper school years. Without it they cannot do justice either to the areas of study or to the religions concerned

One way of helping pupils of the Middle school years to understand something of the authority of scriptures for a religious community is through finding out about the translating of the Bible and the way in which the Bible has been handed down through the centuries. The discovery of biblical mauscripts, especially the Qumran (Dead Sea Scrolls) finds and the story of Tischendorf's discovery of the famous Sinaiticus Manuscript, and the painstaking work done on the thousands of fragments of manuscripts, are fascinating to this age group. So also is the story of the continual task of translation of the Bible into a language that ordinary people can read, particularly the account of the work--and the death—of William Tyndale.

Teachers sometimes try to convince children of the authority of the Bible by telling them that it is a holy book, or the 'Word of God'. Quite apart from the fact that it is only within a community of faith that any scriptures can be described as 'the' Word of God (as they are in Judaism, Christianity and Islam), merely telling pupils is ineffective. Most children of primary school age will believe their teachers, because they are prepared to accept things on the authority of adults, but by about thirteen many of them have developed a strong reaction against the Bible, partly for the very reason that adults have told them that they ought to regard it as a holy book.

Much more valuable are schemes of work on the translation and transmission of the Bible, so that the pupils can discover how it has been important for men and women down the centuries and in the world today. As the pupils grow up they will have to decide what authority, if any, the Bible has for them personally, but in religious education they will be learning something of the importance of the Christian Scriptures within the Christian community of faith.

14

Teaching about Jesus

Teaching about Jesus has been the focal point of all the Agreed Syllabuses: His birth, his ministry, his life, his teaching, his death, his resurrection were all considered appropriate for Infants, for Juniors, for younger Secondaries and for examination papers in C.S.E. and G.C.E. Although the total effect turned out to be more negative than the compilers of the syllabuses intended, at least it was possible to understand this emphasis when the aim of religious education was to communicate the Christian faith or, as it was sometimes expressed in introductions to syllabuses, to 'bring the child into an encounter with Jesus Christ'.

Now that we no longer have this confessional aim, how do we present the person and the teaching of Jesus?

When it was suggested earlier (p.64) that there were particular difficulties in teaching about the founders of religions and that it was not wise to make extended reference to them much before the Upper school stage, it might have been thought that teachers were being asked to reverse the traditional policy and not to mention Jesus in the First and Middle school years. This would of course be both wrong and impossible, and it would be inconsistent with the kind of R.E. whose aim is to help pupils to understand what religion is, particularly through a study of the religion of the country in which they are living.

There are two distinctions which need to be made. First, between references to a founder and study of his life. The former would be appropriate for any of the great religious figures. And secondly, between the founder of the religion which is being studied at greatest depth and the founders of other religions. It would be as unnatural for children in this country to go through school without hearing about Jesus as it would be for children in Buddhist countries not to hear about Gautama or children in Muslim countries not to hear about Muhammad.

To confirm the central place of Jesus in R.E. in this country, however, is not to solve the many difficulties in teaching about him.

There is probably more confusion in children's minds about Jesus than about anything else in the whole of R.E.—in spite of the familiarity of the material through repetition. There are three areas in particular which children find difficult.

First, there is confusion for younger children between Baby Jesus and Jesus the man. This is illustrated by the remark of a six year old whose grandfather had just died. To comfort him his mother said, 'We mustn't worry about Grandad. He's quite happy. He's gone to be with Jesus', only to find herself being asked, 'Is Grandad in the stable?' Children at the Infant school stage know that one day they will grow up; they also know, though not quite so clearly, that their parents were once young. What they cannot do is stand back and 'survey' the process of development from babyhood through to adulthood. This is one reason why the structured syllabus which starts with the nativity stories and works through the one boyhood story to Jesus' baptism and ministry and on to his death and resurrection, is completely wasted on young children. Chronological sequence is irrelevant at this age.

We have already (pp.76 f.) discussed using the imagery of the Christmas stories rather than concentrating on telling the stories, particularly at First school stage, and in the same way reference can often be made to Jesus in conversations and discussions rather than in formal story sessions. Without wanting to imply that the person of Jesus is no different from the figure of Father Christmas, it is possible to use the example of Father Christmas to point out that teachers of young children talk about him quite naturally, and they accept and use children's comments, without feeling that they have to do it always in the form of stories.

For fours to sixes the emphasis should be on Jesus the man, not on Baby Jesus. It is adults who matter most to children at this stage, and no young child gets its sense of security from another child, let alone from a baby. The incidental references at Christmas time to the baby in the manger are less confusing to children when the nativity stories are not being used to introduce a continuous account of Jesus' life.

The other two areas of confusion for children can be discussed together because they overlap. They are confusion between Jesus in Palestine 2,000 years ago and Jesus now, and between Jesus' humanity and his divinity. A six year old once asked, 'How can Jesus be God if he prayed to God?' It is impossible to answer that satisfactorily for a child. It is almost equally impossible to answer it satisfactorily for an adult.

Teaching about Jesus

Scholars wrestle with the problem of the relationship between the Jesus of history and the Christ of faith, and if even theologically inclined adults can produce no easy answers to what it means to speak of Jesus' divinity, we can hardly expect children to be able to understand it.

Learning about Christology (what Christians believe about the person of Christ) belongs in the Upper school, particularly in the unit 'Who was Jesus?' In most schools, however, this is at present an impossible study to undertake because of the confused ideas which the pupils have gathered from their earlier years. Instead of embarking on an enquiry to find out what it was that made the first Christians want to say that Jesus was more than a mere man, pupils are likely to dismiss the question as ridiculous—everyone knew that Jesus was God, he said so himself, the archangel told Mary, the angels told the shepherds, he worked miracles, he rose from the dead, he went up into heaven, etc., etc.

Part of the solution to this problem lies in helping pupils to understand the nature of the literature of the Gospels, and this is a very important part of R.E., but there are also some guidelines as to how we should teach about Jesus so as to avoid the most serious areas of confusion.

For children of about ten and under we should concentrate on Jesus' humanity—presenting him as a man, and not as divine. This is not in any sense anti-Christian. The Christian Church has always maintained that Jesus was fully human. The New Testament insists that Jesus was completely a man, not just disguised as one, and its doctrine of the atonement depends as much on Jesus' full humanity as it does on God's activity.

One of the ways in which children will be helped to understand Jesus' humanity is through the background studies we have already referred to (see pp.90 ff.). To find out about the life of a Jewish boy growing up in Palestine at the time of Jesus is to find out what Jesus' life must have been like, and to realise that he would have gone to school, that he would have had to learn Hebrew, and that he would have gradually learned what was in the Scriptures. As we have seen earlier, teaching about Jesus in his Jewish context is essential if pupils are later to understand the significance of the New Testament.

What kind of picture of the man Jesus are we going to give our pupils? It is reasonable at First school stage to show him as kind and loving and willing to help people, but we are being highly selective in our use of the

Gospels if this is the only picture we present to the nines to elevens. Nobody would have bothered to crucify the Jesus of primary school R.E. The Gospels portray a man who compelled intense loyalty from some people and aroused intense hostility in others. Jesus was the kind of person about whom people felt strongly.

Pupils at the 9—11 stage should be encouraged to think about the kind of person Jesus must have been if, for example, such tough men as fishermen and tax-collectors felt impelled to leave everything that had been important to them and follow a wandering preacher. If the pupils have done background study of life in Palestine in the first century they will know something of the hard life of the fishermen and realise that Simon and Andrew and James and John would be pretty rugged characters. They will also know that tax-collectors were on to a good thing. What would make a hard-bitten tax-collector throw up his attractive income for a life of poverty and insecurity? It certainly wouldn't be loneliness, as versions of the Zacchaeus story for children often suggest. Tax-collectors had plenty of friends; Matthew threw a great party when he became a disciple so that his friends could meet Jesus (Mt. 9:10).

The purpose of this kind of inquiry is to stimulate the pupils to think about the person of Jesus; it is not to impose 'answers' to the questions, or to provide a neat and precise portrait of Jesus. The Gospels present us with an enigmatic figure which eludes any attempt at neat classification.

If primary schools have tended to present Jesus as kind and gentle and loving, secondary schools have tended to present him as the upholder of conventional morality, as the ally of authority, and as the opponent of change. If this sounds too extreme one only needs to look at the way in which Jesus' teaching and actions are used in courses that deal with personal relationships, man in community, work and leisure, etc. While the primary school picture is a partial one, the secondary picture is totally false—almost a complete reversal of the picture in the Gospels. This is partly because we have tended to focus on the *context* in which he was teaching rather than on the *principles* of his teaching. For example, in the parable of the Pharisee and the Publican (Lk. 18:9) emphasis is put on Jesus' condemnation of the Pharisee rather than on his condemnation of self-righteousness, with the ironic result that pupils tend to draw the conclusion 'Thank goodness we are not like the Pharisee'!

It seems doubly sad that Jesus should be presented to adolescents as an establishment figure, first because it was his challenge to so many of the accepted religious and social standards of his day that roused such strong opposition, and secondly, because adolescents are at the stage of psychological development when they respond positively to the real Jesus of the Gospels and negatively to the Jesus of traditional R.E.

One of the reasons why Jesus appears to pupils to be such an innocuous person is that the Gospel stories are often presented in highly simplistic terms. All Jesus' supporters are 'good', all his opponents are 'bad'—wicked, legalistic and hypocritical. It is perhaps not surprising that non-specialist teachers should take this rather stylised approach for it is to a certain extent what is found in the Gospels themselves (though there is no such excuse for people who plan syllabuses or write books for teachers).

The Gospels were written out of a conflict situation and they reflect the bitterness and struggle that surrounded the establishment of the Christian Church. It was not a conflict between two religions, Judaism and Christianity, but between two sections of the same religion, each of which claimed that it represented that religion most truly. It was no accident that the Christians had as their only scriptures the Jewish Bible, that Jews and Christians worshipped the same God, and that Christians saw themselves as heirs to the promises made to Israel. Disagreement about beliefs within a religion (or an ideology or political party) is more intense and more bitter than disagreement between two largely unrelated groups.

This brings us back to two areas we have already discussed—background study and understanding the nature of the literature we are using.

Background study of Judaism enables us to set the incidents recounted in the Gospels in some kind of perspective. We see the Pharisees in a different light when we find that their teaching also condemned hypocrisy and legalism. Their temptation to regard the Law as an end in itself instead of as a means to an end (the right relationship with God) is no different from the temptation that faces Christians today to regard the Church or the Bible or whatever as ends in themselves instead of as means to an end (the right relationship with God). To condemn this confusion of ends and means is not the same thing as condemning every adherent of the religion.

Some consideration of the 'Ethics of the Fathers' (Pirke Aboth) and of the teaching of the great Rabbis like Hillel will be included in the unit

'Sacred Writings', but teachers of the younger age groups should themselves have some familiarity with the Judaism of the New Testament period so that the material they use does justice to Judaism as well as to Christianity. (A useful start can be made with John Bowden's article 'Jewish Religious Life in the First Century A.D.' in *A Source Book of the Bible for Teachers*, ed. R. C. Walton, S.C.M. Press, 1970.)

Background study has to go hand in hand with an understanding of the nature of the Gospels. Traditional R.E. has assumed that the Gospels are biographies of Jesus and that therefore it is possible to select any section just as it stands to give pupils knowledge of what actually happened. At First and Middle school level the differences between the Gospels have been largely ignored, and stories about Jesus have been taken haphazardly from all the Gospels and put together to make a continuous 'life of Jesus'.

The inconsistencies have often been 'explained' to older pupils as similar to eye-witnesses' variant accounts of an accident. Like the whispering game (see p.95) this is a completely false analogy. It doesn't explain the real nature of the Gospels, it obscures it. The Gospels are in no sense like reporters' accounts. It is totally misleading to suggest that the variations are accounted for by lapses of memory or perception.

There are two main reasons for the variations. First, the traditions about Jesus—his teaching and incidents in his life—were used in the early Church for several decades before the first Gospel was written. A missionary preacher would tell his audience some of the things Jesus had said and done, selecting his illustrations according to what he wanted to emphasise to that particular audience. (One can imagine the parable of the Good Samaritan being a popular illustration in Samaria.) In this way a story could easily get detached from its original context.

Secondly, the Gospel writers were not just collectors of stories. They had their own distinctive emphases and themes, and each probably had a particular set of readers in mind. Each selected and arranged his material so that the Gospel as a whole had its own theological slant.

One of the aims of the unit 'Who was Jesus?' is to help pupils to understand how the material about Jesus was used in the life of the Christian community, and to see how the Gospels as we have them came out of this process rather than being the beginning of it. This process cannot be systematically considered much before the age of 13, but we have to take care that our handling of material from the Gospels in the earlier years does not put obstacles in the way of the pupils' later under-standing.

This means, among other things, not working through the Gospels chronologically, thereby giving the impression that we know the exact sequence of the events in the life of Jesus. It also means detaching the Christmas stories from stories about Jesus' ministry.

Any stories about Jesus' ministry which are told at the First school stage should be told from the point of view of one of the characters in it, e.g., Peter or Matthew or Zacchaeus, rather than as direct accounts of 'what happened'. This is true to the New Testament, for what we have in the Gospels reflects the impact Jesus made on people. At the Middle school stage we should keep this approach, but now we should also be helping the pupils to realise that what we have in the Gospels is a collection of the stories which some of the early Christians selected from all the hundreds of things that Jesus must have said and done, because they wanted to share their understanding of Jesus with other people.

The Gospels were written *after* the Resurrection experiences which were the foundation of the Christian faith. The writers therefore presented their material in the light of their faith. They would see no point in doing anything else, for their only purpose was to share their faith. The Gospels therefore also tell us about the faith of the early Church; they are not just reporters' accounts of the life and ministry of Jesus.

This is important in relation to the miracle stories. If we present these as straight historical accounts of 'what happened' we face three main problems. First, young children regard them as examples of magic, parallel to the manipulation of natural laws which they meet in stories of fantasy—to be relegated to the world of make-believe at the stage when they learn to distinguish fact and fantasy. Secondly, they appear to be irrelevant to today. There is no satisfactory answer to the child's question, 'Then why doesn't he make my Granny better?' Thirdly, they reinforce the concept of God's power, understood as 'making things happen', in contrast to the Christian understanding of God's power, which is seen supremely on the cross—power over evil through self-giving love.

Miracle stories are best left until the pupils can look at them in the context of the purpose of the Gospel writers, e.g., the very different use

John makes of miracles, which he calls 'signs' and uses as illustrations of the new life that Jesus brings, from the use of miracles in the Synoptic Gospels, where they are called 'mighty works' and are linked with the confirmation of Jesus as the inaugurator of the messianic age.

Many people who recognise the difficulties involved in teaching miracles at primary level at least feel that they are on safe ground with parables. However, even these are not without their problems. In the first place, the parable is not an easy literary form for children to understand. In contrast to the allegory, it makes only one main point and the rest of the details are there to make it a good story, not to convey the teaching. This is why we get into such difficulties with parables like the Labourers in the Vineyard (Mt. 20) or the Unjust Steward (Lk. 16) or even the story of the man of doubtful honesty who found treasure hidden in a field and didn't tell the owner of the field (Mt. 13:44).

Secondly, the parables were originally addressed to adults, and many of them just don't speak to children's experience. We have already noted the way in which the parable of the Prodigal Son can speak of a neglectful father rather than a loving one (p.23). Another parable which looks straightforward is the Sower. Of course some children are 'choked with the cares and riches of this world', but the rebuke of the parable should be addressed to their parents, not to the children themselves. And many children do start things with enthusiasm and then give them up, but this is a characteristic of childhood, and particularly of the less able child, and the last thing we should want is to suggest that Jesus' teaching is directed against them.

There are one or two parables which are good as stories. The Lost Sheep (Lk. 15), for example, can convey a positive meaning of caring to young children. But a much more valuable way into the parables is through background schemes. For example, they meet the parable of the Sower when they have learned about the life of the farmer; they then look at a story Jesus told about a farmer. In this way the emphasis is put on the factual details and not on the 'meaning'. Consideration of the meaning belongs at secondary level.

Finally, a word about honesty. This is not a criticism of teachers, for most of them are completely unaware of any dishonesty in their approach, and they are very much at the mercy of the textbooks. However, when we are teaching about Jesus we must be on our guard against the temptation to demonstrate his importance by making claims for his originality which are not true to the facts. For instance, we are accustomed to talk about the contrast between the Jewish Ten Commandments and Jesus' two commandments. This must be very frustrating for members of the Jewish community who know that 'Thou shalt love the Lord thy God . . .' is in their Scriptures (Deut. 6:4f) and so is 'Thou shalt love thy neighbour as thyself' (Lev. 19:18). We should also notice that in one of the Gospels the words are actually put into the mouth of a Jewish lawyer and not of Jesus (Lk. 10:25f).

Similarly there is a tendency to suggest that the fact that Jesus performed miracles proves his divinity. Miracle-working was actually a commonly accepted phenomenon in the first century (a Greek expression for miracle workers was 'sons of God'). And even within the Gospels we find a reference to the Pharisees casting out demons (Mt. 12:27).

This is not in any sense advocating a policy of playing down the importance of Jesus. It is merely the recognition that no cause, however worthy, is well served by inaccuracy. And far from having a negative effect, the total approach which has been outlined is much more likely to encourage pupils at secondary level to take the person of Jesus seriously and to study with some degree of understanding what Christians believe about him.

15

Worship . . .

There are two quite distinct ways in which worship comes into a consideration of religious education. The first is as a central element in the study of religion, the second is as an experience provided for pupils, normally in the context of the statutory act of worship.

We shall start by looking at what is involved in helping pupils to understand worship, as part of the total aim of helping them to understand the nature of religion. This is perhaps one of the most difficult areas in the subject, for worship lies at the very heart of a religion and it can well be argued that unless one is actually a worshipper in a particular religion one cannot know what worship means within that religious tradition. We are even more obviously 'on the outside' when considering the worship of a religion than we are when considering its history, its institutions, its sacred writings or even its system of beliefs. However, although it is impossible to get 'inside' the worship of another faith, there are things we can do which make possible a considerable degree of understanding.

We come back once again to the principle of gradually building up understanding. We shall certainly fail in our purpose if we try to teach pupils of any age—even sixth formers—about worship in religions without considerable preparatory studies. What should these preparatory studies involve?

First, with younger pupils we must as always start with the concrete and the observable. In a multi-faith school this will mean, as we have already seen (pp. 68 f.) children talking about what they *do*, in particular in relation to festivals. For some festivals this will involve going to the Gurdwara or the Synagogue or the Church. It might also mean that the children talk about the Punjabi or Hebrew or Arabic classes they go to outside school hours. This can help the rest of the class to realise the importance of the language not only in the family but in worship and in the reading of the Scriptures.

The unit 'Sacred Places' for the Middle school years takes a more systematic look at the kinds of building associated with worship in different religions. One of the purposes of this study is to help the pupils to realise that there are differences not only in the structure of the buildings but in the ways in which they are used, the role of sacred writings, the functions of the officials, etc. By the end of this unit pupils should be quite clear that the word 'worship' does not have only one meaning, and that one cannot make a straightforward transfer from Christianity to other religions. They should know, for example, that Jews and Christians have weekly congregational services which normally include prayers, readings from the Scriptures, hymns and a sermon, Muslims go to the Mosque at midday on Friday to say together the prayers which they would otherwise be saying on their own, while Hindus visit their Temples individually and not for congregational worship.

However, they should also have discovered that the picture isn't quite as simple as that. In the first place there are variations within each religion. Secondly, members of a religious order in any faith have a different pattern of worship which tends to be more frequent and more disciplined than that of the layman. And thirdly, when a religious community is a minority group in an alien culture there are bound to be some changes in its way of life. For example, in India there are a number of Hindu temples in any town or city and there are always people in them, making their individual prayers and offerings. In Britain there are few temples, and these are mainly small buildings which have to remain closed during the week because the community cannot support the staff to keep them open. Instead, Hindus in Britain tend to meet on Sunday for a service of worship followed by a communal meal. This serves as a focal point for the Hindu community in an area. They meet on Sunday not because it is a holy day but because it is the one day in the week when working people are free to meet.

A deeper knowledge of the character of the main religions will be gained through the unit 'Festivals'. Festivals are concerned with those features of a religion which it regards as particularly significant, and although the emphasis in the unit will not be on worship in the narrow sense, an understanding of what is regarded as most significant in a religion is absolutely essential if its worship is not to be misunderstood. For example, a study of the Jewish festival of Passover, in which events

109

of the past are brought into dynamic and creative relationship with the present, helps us to interpret rightly the place given in Jewish worship to events of long ago.

Because sacred writings play an important part in the worship of the five major religions represented in Britain, the pupils' increasing knowledge of the nature and authority of these writings will make a certain contribution to their understanding of the religions' worship.

But absolutely central to understanding worship is knowledge of what the worshipper believes about the object of his worship and how he views his relationship with the God he worships. For example, let us imagine someone in another faith setting out to learn about Christian worship. If he has not first learned that central to Christianity is the belief that the relationship of God to man is best expressed in terms of fatherhood and love and the offer of forgiveness and new life, he might well interpret the words of the General Confession, especially the reference to being 'miserable offenders', as an indication that Christians worshipped an angry deity who had to be placated. Finding out about the words spoken in worship is not the same thing as understanding what the worship means.

It is mainly because a reasonable degree of maturity is needed to understand without distortion a religion's beliefs about its deity or deities that any direct study of worship must come at a fairly late stage in a pupil's study of religion.

Through their studies the pupils will be discovering the universal nature of worship. With the exception of some forms of Buddhism it exists in every religion. They should also be discovering that the impulse to worship is a basic human characteristic and not confined to members of religious communities, even though the objects of worship may be as diverse as a national hero or a pop idol or football or money.

They will learn that although worship is a universal phenomenon in religion, it takes different forms in different faiths and that there are variations within different religions. It is not easy in this country to help pupils to understand what the differences are within other faiths, but the nature of variations can be illustrated from a study of groups within Christianity. There should therefore be some consideration not only of the similarities and differences in Roman Catholic, Anglican and Free Church worship but of the worship of, say, the Eastern Orthodox Church, the Society of Friends and the charismatic movements. Something of the form of the service, especially of the first three groups, would come into the Middle school years, where it would be related to the architecture of the buildings and their furnishings. The study of the other groups belongs more appropriately in the Upper school, unless they come within the experience of the pupils, when they would naturally be included earlier.

The statutory act of worship in schools has sometimes been defended on the grounds that one cannot understand a religion without experiencing its worship. There is some truth in this, but it is not as straightforward as it sounds.

On this argument a form of religious education that includes the study of a number of religions would require a school to provide acts of worship of all the religions being studied. Quite apart from the fact that this could easily become an artificial exercise, only the pupils who were adherents of the religion being represented on a particular day would actually be having any experience of worship. The others would be merely spectators, watching actions and hearing words, but certainly not identified with the worship being offered.

Regular assemblies of this nature would be utterly confusing to children at the primary school stage. They might be interested to discover what different things were done in different religions, but that is an experience of learning about something, it is not by the wildest stretch of the imagination an experience of worship.

Worship in any religion (with the exception of meditation in some forms of Buddhism) is an activity of response, the response of the worshipper to the deity he worships. 'Worship' is a transitive verb—we must worship something or someone. For worship to take place there must be some sort of concept of the object of worship, and there must be an act of commitment in which the worshipper acknowledges a relationship between himself and the object of his worship. Worship therefore belongs only within a community of faith.

We need not spend any time on the idea of a composite act of worship. It is possible to compile an anthology of prayers and readings taken from different religions, and this can be extremely valuable for study purposes or for reflecting on the wisdom of the faiths of man. It might be suitable for an occasional assembly but it would not be teaching the pupils about the worship of any religion and it would certainly not be providing an experience of worship for them.

At the stage when pupils are studying worship as part of their religious education they should have the opportunity to attend services of worship of different religious traditions. In this situation an act of worship in school, taken either by pupils or by someone from outside, can be helpful. Even better, however, are visits to actual places of worship. Where this is part of a scheme of study, and sufficient preparatory work has been done, the actual experience of sharing with the worshipping community in its own setting will convey more effectively than anything else what worship is like for the adherents of that religion. The pupils will still be 'on the outside' but this is probably the nearest they can get to glimpsing what being 'on the inside' might mean. It must be emphasised, however, that a visit by itself is not enough. If the pupils have not done the kind of preparatory studies outlined in the first part of this chapter, they are likely to gain little more than an acquaintance with the outward form of the worship.

Most of the defenders of the statutory act of worship in schools have argued for it not on the grounds of its contribution to the study of religions but because they considered that pupils should have an experience of worship. It has sometimes been claimed that the school should provide this experience because the pupils would otherwise not get it as so few of them go to church. This raises a number of issues.

First, the school is not an arm of the Christian Church. The Church, like the other religious communities, is a voluntary body. Its members have the option of belonging or not belonging. The schools are statutory bodies. They are the schools of the whole community and, up to the age of 16, their members do not have the option of not belonging. (One recognises the different position of the denominational schools. Roman Catholic schools exist to provide a certain kind of education for Roman Catholic children and they are therefore not the schools of the whole community. The situation in relation to Anglican schools is not so clear-cut. Although they are Church schools, they are often the only schools in an area, and where this is the case they are community schools.) The maintained school's function is different from that of the religious community, and it must not act as if it is part of the community of faith.

As we have seen, worship is a responsive activity and it has meaning only within a context of faith. Worship involves commitment. If it is not right in the community's schools to attempt to initiate pupils into a

particular religion, then it can hardly become right, just because they
have left their classrooms and gone into the hall, to assume that they
are members of a particular religion and expect them to worship the
God of that religion.

The second issue raised by the argument for the statutory act of
worship is not whether we should give children an experience of worship
in school, but whether we can. If the verb 'worship' is transitive, and
involves worshipping someone or something, who or what are the pupils
from non-Christian homes 'worshipping'? They may be co-operative
enough to join in the prayers, but who are they 'praying' to? Children
from Christian homes could well be having an experience of worship in
the traditional assembly, but it is the others for whom the act of worship
is often defended as a necessary experience.

We can take this reasoning a stage further. Pupils who come from
non-religious homes (especially homes where 'God' and 'Jesus' are
merely swearwords) are not only not getting an experience of Christian
worship, but they are building up concepts of the Christian God which
could put them off wanting to worship him or make them want to
worship him for the wrong reasons—and if it is not the task of the
school to teach for belief, neither is its task to put obstacles in the way
of belief.

All worship involves beliefs about the deity who is being worshipped.
What ideas might children from non-religious homes get from traditional
school worship, especially in the First and Middle school?

They could get the idea that God is someone you talk to—which
would, of course, be an accurate understanding of what Christians
believe—but it is apparently a one-way conversation. And you shut
your eyes when you speak to him. Then you thank him for all the good
things of life—but who sends the bad things? Then you ask him for
things, particularly those things you can't get any other way—but why
doesn't he always give them to you when you ask?

This may sound like a caricature, for at the primary stage children
are ready to accept what adults tell them and only a minority will be
consciously worried about traditional assembly—or traditional R.E.
It is in early adolescence, when they are organising and integrating their
experience, that they question what they have had on the authority of
adults, especially when it doesn't square with their own experience. By
the time they reach 13 many pupils refuse even to discuss Christian

beliefs. They combine—oddly—a refusal to believe that God exists because he doesn't answer prayers, with a rejection of him because he allows the innocent to suffer. There are of course other reasons for adolescents' rejection of the Christian religion, but if we put ourselves into the situation of the primary school child from a non-religious home we can understand at least one source of the later ideas.

There is another sense in which the traditional school assembly gives pupils a misleading idea of worship. For the committed believer, worship is the response of the whole of his life; what we call an 'act of worship' is a formal expression of that total response. The pupil who thinks that Christian worship is just 'hymns and prayers and readings from the Bible' has completely missed its real significance.

The one form of Christian worship which does give some idea of the hinterland that lies behind it is the Communion service—the Eucharist, which is at the heart of worship in mainstream Christianity. It is structured to express the faith of the worshipper much more comprehensively than the so-called 'hymn sandwich'. But it is not likely to communicate its real meaning to the outsider (certainly not when the outsider is a child), and it is the act of worship which, above all others, assumes commitment on the part of those participating in it.

We recognised earlier that pupils studying other religions could not expect to get on the 'inside' of the worship of these religions, and that they had to undertake considerable preparatory study of a religion if they were not to misunderstand its worship. A large number of pupils in our schools are in the same situation in relation to the Christian religion. Some of them are active members of other faiths, some have a nodding acquaintance with the Christian Church, but many are growing up in virtual isolation from it, and we have to structure their learning about it as carefully as we have to structure their learning about the other major religions.

It has been suggested in this chapter that the study of worship is a highly important part of religious education but that a regular act of worship is not an appropriate activity in the community's schools. What then do we do about Assembly?

16

... Assembly

In the previous chapter we looked at the reasons which led us to question the traditional act of worship in schools. Two main reasons were discussed. First, the illogicality of putting pupils of all faiths and none into a position of commitment and expecting them to offer worship to the Christian God. Secondly, the recognition that the presence of pupils at a service of worship is no guarantee that they are getting either an experience of worship or an insight into what worship is.

There is of course statutory provision for pupils to be withdrawn from the act of worship, and some have argued that worship should be voluntary, at least for senior pupils. But school assembly is much more than a Church service which happens to be held in the school hall. It is a coming together of a community and it should therefore be inclusive, not exclusive. Assembly, like religious education, must be a valid educational experience for *all* pupils.

It might be argued that once assembly ceases to be a specific act of worship it is of no more interest to R.E. However, as an expression of the life and concerns of the community and as an exploration of the experiences which are significant to the pupils, it can make an important contribution to R.E., though on the implicit and not on the explicit side.

What are the characteristics of an assembly that provides a valid and essential educational experience for all pupils? Some or all of these characteristics can already be found in many schools, especially at primary level.

First and most important, assembly is taken by the pupils who, instead of preparing a conventional service, share with the rest of the school something that they have been learning about. This means the end of the desperate search for a theme that is considered 'suitable' for a religious occasion (with the consequent repetition of Courage and Kindness and Giving and Helping and Thankfulness). The subject of the assembly will normally be something which comes out of the immediate experience of the pupils—perhaps a school journey or other activity, but more often a topic they have been working on in class. The criterion for choosing a subject for assembly is whether the pupils enjoyed the experience and were stimulated to think about it sufficiently to want to share it with others. There is thus no topic which is ruled out in advance as 'unsuitable'.

To have an assembly arising out of work done in class is relatively easy in First and some Middle schools; it takes much more careful organisation in schools which have subject teachers rather than class teachers. However, older pupils are less likely to want to base assemblies on their work in school. There may be occasions when this is appropriate, especially in relation to integrated studies, but more often they will want to explore questions about life and experience and the meaning of man's existence, and a system whereby a section of a class or a group of friends from different classes can arrange to take assembly is probably best at this level.

Among the younger age groups, the practice of basing assembly on work that is being done in the classroom means that its preparation is no longer an extra activity that takes up time which would normally be devoted to other things. It now becomes integrated into the normal work of the school, and the discussion about what is to go into an assembly can be a useful exercise in both reinforcement and discrimination.

However, every assembly should be carefully thought out and prepared for, and it is obvious that no class could be expected to produce a good assembly once a week or once a fortnight. Each school therefore has to consider how frequently it should have assembly. Quality is much more important than quantity. A school with a large number of classes could obviously have assemblies more often than a small school, but the criterion will always be the quality of the experience which the pupils will have.

This criterion must be applied to size as well as to frequency. One argument for having the whole school together is that it creates a sense of unity. However, it is possible that the sense of unity is more apparent to the teachers than to the pupils. For the under sevens, the unit of 'belonging' is the class, not the school, and five year olds could well find the 'big boys and girls' quite overpowering. In a village school where the families know each other and the whole school population is not large, the children—five year olds as well as ten year olds—might well get a sense of unity from the coming together of the whole community. This would be much less likely in a larger school in an urban area.

There is another factor to be taken into consideration. In no other aspect of education do we think that what is right for five year olds or even seven year olds is also right for eleven year olds, and no lesson or discussion deemed appropriate for eleven year olds would be used in the sixth form. There may be other advantages to be gained from occasionally bringing such separated age groups together, but if assembly is to serve the purpose of stimulating pupils' thinking and imagination and deepening their understanding, then it is obvious that on most occasions we shall need a narrower age band.

Most JMI schools keep their Infant and Junior assemblies separate; some bring the whole school together once a month for a special assembly. Some primary schools put only two or three classes together so that the children who are responsible for the assembly have a reasonably-sized group of approximately their own age and interests with whom to share what they have been learning about.

Experiments at secondary level include year groups, two year and three year bands, and separate sixth form assemblies. House assemblies are an attempt to make a smaller unit and provide a sense of community within a house but these also run into the problems of a wide age range.

Separate assemblies for the sixth form are very important indeed. The type of work being done at this level, and the fact that the pupils are involved in making decisions about their future, mean that they will want to explore many issues which are not yet seen as urgent by younger pupils.

Sixth form colleges are very well placed to provide opportunities for their students to reflect on the questions of meaning that confront man and to express the values and the concerns of the college community. One sixth form college had a weekly assembly which anyone, staff or students, could volunteer to take. An hour was set aside for the assembly plus tutor groups and the actual assembly could take as much or as little of that hour as those presenting it wanted. There was no set pattern for the assembly, which took a wide variety of forms.

The time of assembly is another question which each school must discuss in relation to its own situation. First thing in the morning is probably the least suitable time. What makes a school a community is that it functions as a community—showing the characteristics of belonging, sharing, interdependence, etc., and any feeling the pupils have that the school is a community is likely to emerge during the day; it is not likely to be something they are particularly conscious of at 9.00 a.m.

In addition to this, if the pupils are sharing in assembly something they have been doing in class, they will find it much easier to make their final preparations on the day itself rather than on the previous day. The younger the children the more important this is.

There is one reason why a First school might decide to have some assemblies either first thing in the morning or last thing in the afternoon, and that is so that the mothers, or whoever brings the children to school, can attend. Some schools welcome mothers at every assembly, some have an 'open' assembly once a week or once a month. There are schools which have been doing this for so long that they now have as pupils children who have been coming to the school with their mothers once a week since they were babies!

There are occasions when other members of the school community—caretakers, cleaners, kitchen helpers, 'lollipop' men or women—might also be invited to come to assembly. And members of the wider community might sometimes be invited. For example, children can more easily develop natural relationships with such people as policemen and recreation ground superintendents if they have invited them to assembly and acted as hosts to them.

The question of visitors is raised in a different way for Church schools. Traditionally one of the clergy takes assembly once a week. This is seldom a satisfactory situation for anyone and it is particularly unsatisfactory at First or Middle school level. It is a cruelly tough assignment for the parson. No one who comes into a school community from outside can relate in any significant way to the work and the concerns of the children. Even someone who is 'good with children' (and the training of the clergy gives them little opportunity to develop this aspect of their ministry) cannot communicate effectively with such a wide age range, and all that we know about children suggests that sitting listening to an adult constitutes just about the worst possible conditions for learning.

In some Church schools the clergy have changed their role and they see their responsibility in pastoral and not in instructional terms—listening rather than talking. They still come to assembly, but as ordinary members of the community, to listen and, incidentally, to learn what are the real interests and concerns of the children.

One of the fears sometimes voiced about assembly being taken by the pupils is that classes might compete with each other to see which can put on the best 'performance'. This would of course be disastrous, but there are two points which can be made. The first can be dealt with very briefly. Where the general ethos of a school is competitive, it will be difficult to keep this spirit out of assembly, but that is a reflection of the values of the school as a whole and not a necessary accompaniment of this kind of assembly.

The second point is that where the activity is seen as *sharing* something with others, the emphasis will be put on those on the receiving end rather than on those leading assembly. This is relevant in the preparation as well as in the presentation. For example, pupils who have been doing a topic for two or three weeks will need to decide which are the best things to select from all that they have learned so that the rest of the pupils will get a clear picture and not be confused. This is a very useful exercise in discrimination and communication.

When it comes to the presentation the pupils should also be thinking about others. Practising in the hall, with some of the class at the back to test audibility, becomes concern for those at the back rather than an elocution lesson. And trying out visual material and making the discovery that it wouldn't be seen by anyone sitting more than five rows from the front is an important experience for children. Being told the same fact by the teacher is no substitute for this experience, which, among other things, is helping children to put themselves in other people's shoes (see p.11).

If there is no set pattern for assembly the pupils are more likely to use their ingenuity to overcome difficulties. For example, the children who discover that their paintings are too small to be seen further back than five rows may decide that they have enough paintings which illustrate the point they want to make to put them at intervals round the walls so that everyone can see at least one painting clearly.

One school which takes seriously the role of communication in assembly makes use of a large display board in one of its main corridors. The class whose turn it is to take assembly puts up in advance an indication of its theme. Sometimes this takes the form of a straightforward announcement of the theme, with some illustrations from the class's topic work; sometimes it is in a more enigmatic form, with either just visual material, or one or more questions. The rest of the school take a great interest in the display. It stimulates discussion, and the children come to assembly with a sense of anticipation to find out more rather than just as passive listeners. It is also a great help to the children taking the assembly if they don't have to 'start from cold'.

Another characteristic of the kind of assembly we are discussing is the much more varied use it makes of the creative arts—painting, music, dance, etc. The atmosphere they can evoke is an important ingredient in assembly. Our traditional assemblies have been almost entirely cerebral activities—talking and listening. This emphasis on intellectual understanding puts younger children and less able pupils at a serious disadvantage, but at any level of ability it is too restricted and unbalanced an approach—and it contrasts strangely with the kind of learning experiences provided in most primary schools. Both the pupils taking assembly and those who are attending need the opportunity to express what they feel—and what we feel can seldom be expressed adequately in words.

The music used at assembly, especially at First and Middle school level, will be mainly the pupils' own composition, e.g., music using percussion instruments, created to illustrate some aspect of the topic, or words which have been put to a familiar tune, but there are some songs, especially folk songs and even the ephemeral pop songs, which quite young children respond to, and which express what children and young people feel much more authentically than the traditional hymns ever did.

Finally, it is perhaps important to point out how an assembly in which the pupils explore and reflect upon their experience can actually include most if not all of the basic elements of worship, even though it uses no religious language and has no hymns or prayers.

One of the main elements in worship is awe or wonder. For the small child this is usually evoked by some experience of natural beauty—a flower, a butterfly, etc. It is a spontaneous response, usually to something that is small in size, and it cannot therefore be organised as part of assembly for the under sevens. But for the sevens to twelves awe and wonder are evoked more by factual knowledge about how things work, whether it is the movement of the planets, the construction of the human body, or the functioning of a coal mine, and pupils of this age will naturally include in their assembly the kind of information which has made them want to say to someone, 'Did you know that . . .?'

For the thirteen plus age group interest is likely to be directed mainly towards persons and questions of meaning, and as a result awe and wonder will be less obvious ingredients of assembly for this age group.

A related element—thanksgiving—will also predominate more in the First and Middle school years. This will not take the form of prayers of thanksgiving addressed to a deity. It will rather be that activity which comes so naturally to children—the expression of sheer joy and delight in the world in which they find themselves and in what they have done and what they have discovered.

In traditional school worship both prayers of confession and prayers asking for the strength to do what is right have seemed to many pupils suspiciously like an extension of authority's concern for discipline in the school (could they be right?). In the kind of assembly we are talking about there would be occasions when the pupils would express their recognition that man has done things which have brought suffering to others, e.g., in the misuse of natural resources, in pollution, in conflict between groups. This emphasis is less appropriate with younger children; it will increase through the Middle school years and will predominate in the Upper school.

Similarly, concern for those who suffer hardship will be expressed differently by different age groups. Six year olds taking an assembly on Winter, for example, would quite naturally tell how they break the ice each morning on the bird table so that the birds can have something to drink. Older children who did a class topic on Winter might have included a study of people whose work was particularly hazardous in winter—mountain rescue teams, lifeboatmen, trawlermen, etc.—and they would talk about this in their assembly. And the very real sympathy of adolescents for the oppressed and those who are lonely or homeless or starving will find frequent expression in their assemblies. Prayers of intercession would not be used but the basic element in intercession—the identification with and concern for those in need—would be part of assembly.

We could make more use of silence in assembly than we normally do. 'Stillness' is perhaps a better word than silence. It suggests a positive activity of reflection. But if pupils are to be still they must be given something worth thinking about, and preferably something to look at. Closing one's eyes is for many children synonymous with thinking about something quite different!

This last point is just one more illustration of the fact that the conventions of school worship have prevented us from using in assembly all the educational knowledge which is applied so effectively in the classroom. Those schools which have managed to free themselves from such restraints and have put the needs of the pupils first, have discovered that assembly has 'come to life' and become an experience which has a great deal to offer not only to the individuals participating in it, but to the whole life of the school community.

17

Integrating religious education

It was a tragedy for religious education that the sudden growth of interest in integrated studies came at a time when the subject itself was in a state of such confusion.

At the secondary level some schools were keeping firmly to their Bible-based syllabuses, and their contribution to integrated studies therefore tended to take the form of 'relevant' passages from the Bible. Other schools were adopting the problem-centred approach and their contribution tended to be thought of in terms of discussing moral issues. The situation was no clearer in the primary school. Even teachers who used life-themes still included Bible stories and, as we have seen (p.25) these came to be regarded as the religious part of the theme. As a result biblical material was considered to be the appropriate R.E. element in class projects or topics.

By the end of the sixties, however, there had been a more widespread move away from the use of the Bible, and religious education came increasingly to be thought of as concerned with moral values. Many primary school teachers, when asked about their R.E., said cheerfully, 'Oh, it's in everything we do'. Many secondary school teachers had reshaped their syllabuses, at least for the thirteen-plus classes, to centre on personal, social and international issues, and they welcomed with open arms the materials which came from the Schools Council Humanities and Moral Education Projects.

These were often lively teachers, men and women who were acutely aware of the negative results produced by the conventional R.E. syllabuses, and who had the courage to change the pattern of their own teaching. They were, for the same reasons, often in the forefront of experiments in integrated studies. However, it was the stage of development through which religious education was passing in the sixties which meant that many an integrated study turned out to be the quicksands in which R.E. sank without trace.

This is one of the reasons why religious education is now so often equated with moral education. It was assumed, and rightly, that one doesn't need to be a religious education specialist to encourage pupils to explore the human aspects of whatever topic is under discussion. This understanding of the subject found practical, if disastrous, expression in the omission in many middle and secondary schools of a religious education member of a humanities or general studies team.

How different should the role of R.E. be in integrated work when the subject is interpreted as it has been in this book?

The clue lies in the aim of religious education. If some aspect of a topic is helping pupils to understand the nature of religion, then that topic is making a contribution to religious education—or, seen the other way round, religious education is making a contribution within the topic. But, as we have seen, that is an ultimate aim, to be achieved only by the end of the secondary school, and for practical purposes we have to be able to think clearly about the various objectives which have to be achieved if we are to have any hope of achieving the ultimate aim.

To take one example, pupils must be able to understand the role of sacred writings in religion and, more specifically, they must know that there are different kinds of literature in sacred writings. This involves a fairly detailed consideration of the literature of the Judaeo-Christian Scriptures. The way in which this understanding is built up within religious education has been discussed in previous chapters (chapters 12—14), but let us see in what ways it might be associated with other aspects of the curriculum.

Anything that helps children to recognise and appreciate different kinds of literature—poetry (and different kinds of poetry: ballad, non-sense verse, epic, etc.), stories (and the difference between stories with a historical basis, fairy stories, folk tales, legends, myths, pure fiction, biography, autobiography, etc.), historical documents (and the difference between personal letters, political pamphlets, newspaper reports, parish records, etc.)—is laying the kind of foundation which is needed for recognising different kinds of literature in sacred writings.

More explicitly, a topic on 'Books' for the nines to elevens could include a section on the discoveries of biblical manuscripts (e.g., at Mount Sinai and Qumran); or the glories of the illuminated manuscripts which were produced with such painstaking care in monasteries; or the nature of scrolls in the biblical period, with their approximate length of

30 feet, which meant that they often contained more than one writing (e.g., the writings of the unknown prophet of the Jewish Exile, added to those of Isaiah of Jerusalem—with the division coming after chapter 39 in the Book of Isaiah); or the fact that when codices (i.e., books with pages) were invented, near the beginning of our era, it was the Christian Church which took them up with the greatest enthusiasm because 'using' the Scriptures was very important to a group which put so much emphasis on its continuity with the past, and it was much easier to find a passage by turning the pages of a book than unrolling a 30 foot scroll.

If a topic on 'Books' was being done with tens to twelves it would be possible to include a fairly substantial section on the world's 'best-seller'—the Bible. This would probably include something of the story of its translation down the centuries and the continuing work of translation into a more modern form of English as well as into over a thousand other languages.

Pupils in the Middle and Upper school should also be helped to recognise the influence of the Bible in language and literature, e.g., through the numerous expressions which have entered our language— 'the apple of his eye', 'to draw a bow at a venture', 'to turn the other cheek', 'the prodigal returns', etc.—and the frequent allusions in literature, many of them incidental but many others indicating the meaning of the work as a whole—*Eyeless in Gaza* by Aldous Huxley, *The Rainbow* by D. H. Lawrence, etc. (And pupils reading *Paradise Lost* should make the discovery that Milton's account of the origin of evil comes not from the Old Testament but from the intertestamental period.) This should happen incidentally in English but it might receive more systematic treatment in an integrated course on 'Man in Society' which included some consideration of the cultural heritage of our society.

Another objective in religious education is to enable the pupils to recognise the different ways in which language is used in religion, particularly its symbolic use. As with our first example we can see that anything which helps pupils to handle language with some confidence and to realise that the same words may have different meanings—sometimes a metaphorical as well as a literal meaning—is making an important contribution to religious education. So also is the kind of study we have just been describing in relation to different kinds of literature.

In a more systematic way, units like 'Signs and Symbols' and 'Asking

Questions' help pupils to think more clearly about the different uses of language. These units have been suggested for R.E. because this kind of study is absolutely essential for understanding the nature of religion, but they would also make excellent topics for integrated courses. Where a school makes special provision for such courses they would obviously be good candidates for inclusion, but even where there are no integrated studies a great deal can be done if colleagues in different departments are prepared to plan together and to arrange sections of their syllabus so that although the pupils apparently follow a formal compartmented timetable, they are taking up different aspects of the same topic in two or more subjects. Even where another department doesn't feel that the topic warrants full scale treatment, it might be prepared to devote a smaller amount of time to it. This might apply in 'Asking Questions'. A science department might see that there were real advantages in getting pupils to think about the kinds of questions that are asked at different levels of science, and about the nature of the scientists' 'answers', though they might feel that this should be incidental to the physics or biology course in progress.

An integrated studies course on 'Communication' could include a section on signs and symbols. One on 'Barriers' could include a consideration of the barriers between men which are created by the fact that language is not a precise tool, and words can be interpreted in different ways depending on the experience or the cultural background of the person who hears or reads them.

An Upper school integrated course on 'Communication' for more academic pupils could include a study of the way in which language is used within different discourses of meaning, and this would involve a study of the uses of language in religion.

A third objective in religious education is to help the pupils to understand the place of institutions in religion. Any integrated course which involves the study of a particular country should automatically consider the role of its religious institutions, both nationally and in the lives of ordinary people. To ignore these means that the pupils get only a partial understanding of the country, and the conclusions they draw from their study about its culture, attitudes, values, etc., will therefore not be wholly accurate.

Senior pupils studying such areas as the Indian sub-continent or the Middle East or South East Asia, or individual countries such as Turkey or Israel, will be learning about the religious institutions of one or more of the other world faiths. For most of the time, however, and certainly in the younger age groups, they will learn about aspects of the Christian Church. It is very much easier to understand a social institution when one can see it *in situ*—in its own society, and there are numerous ways in which the Christian Church can enter into integrated studies in addition to those religious education units which focus specifically on it.

First school children, for instance, doing 'Homes and Families', will be discussing their own experience, and where this includes a family going to the local church (or synagogue or mosque or temple) it will naturally feature in the child's work. Sevens to elevens doing a neighbourhood study will take in the local church (or churches, and in some areas the synagogue or mosque or temple). They may look at the Church's activities in the community, and any projects further afield that it supports. They may find out about the symbolism of its characteristic architecture and furnishings and decoration. If it is an old established church they may discover something about its role in the community in earlier ages. Senior pupils doing an integrated course on 'Community' might include such experiments as the Iona and Taizé Communities.

Middle school pupils doing the Elizabethans or Upper school pupils doing the Renaissance or the Victorian age would also be looking at the role of the Christian Church. In this kind of study we need to remind ourselves that it is a great temptation to generalise when we are dealing with past ages (or other cultures). There has probably never been a period in history when there were no exceptions to the dominant image of the Church. For example, in the Darwinian controversy as in the controversy over Galileo's claims two centuries earlier, there were members of the Christian Church on both sides and there were scientists on both sides.

We have used sacred writings, the use of language in religion, and religious institutions to illustrate how, if one has one's R.E. aims clear, one can see the ways in which the subject can be integrated with other aspects of the curriculum. It is this clarity of thinking which will prevent the awful dragging in of material merely because of its verbal associations— as in the familiar 'Jesus' fishermen friends' for a topic on the Sea, or the story of Noah for a topic on Water, or 'Transport in the Bible' for a topic on Transport.

127

This does not mean that an integrated course must never include biblical material. As we saw in relation to human experience themes (pp.30 ff.), the Bible is not to be uncritically banned any more than it is to be uncritically used. The key factor is always whether the biblical material serves to deepen and extend the pupils' understanding of the subject of the integrated course. We have to ask ourselves whether we should want to use the material if it were not in the Bible.

If Upper school pupils were studying 'Man in Society' it would be quite relevant to find out about and discuss ancient Israel's 'welfare state' provisions for the poor, the fatherless and the widows, and its practical concern for the foreigners living in Israelite towns. Or they might discuss the injunctions addressed to Christians in the Sermon on the Mount.

At primary school level a biblical image theme (see pp.92–3) might be linked with a topic. For example, as part of a general study on Water it would be appropriate to have a section that dealt with the way of life of a people whose life quite literally depended on water. Although it would be possible to choose any one of a number of countries to illustrate this, life in Bible times (and in the same countries today) is an essential part of R.E. and therefore of the curriculum, and so would have a strong claim to be included here. The important thing is that the pupils should be absolutely clear about what they are studying at any one time—whether it is the water supply system in this country now, or the huge underground cisterns used two thousand years ago on the rock fortress of Masada, or the new towns in the Negev in southern Israel today whose total water supply is piped across the desert from the river Jordan.

What of that element which was so widely assumed to be religious education's contribution to integrated studies—moral values?

The kind of religious education described in this book is certainly not unconcerned with morality, but it recognises a clear distinction between, on the one hand, a study of the place of morality in religion, especially the relationship between belief and life and, on the other hand, the moral education of the pupils. The latter is the shared responsibility of all the teachers in a school—with the most important factor being the ethos of the school itself. One of the great weaknesses of the traditional teaching of morality through R.E. was that if the pupils rejected the Christian faith—and in adolescence they did so in large numbers—they frequently rejected the morality that had been based on it.

The distinctive task of religious education in relation to morality lies in helping the pupils to understand the relationship of codes of ethics to belief systems. We have already referred to this in the discussion on biographies (p.34) and it would also be dealt with in a systematic way in the unit 'Belief and Life'. It could come into the study of a country or group of countries, where it would be important to see practices and attitudes in the light of the dominant beliefs—Marxist, Hindu, Muslim, etc. And for senior pupils it would be important to understand the tension created where two or more belief systems are held by a considerable number of people, e.g., Marxism and the traditional religion of the country in Italy, parts of India, some of the Latin American countries, etc.

The unit 'What is Man?' has been suggested for religious education because it forms an integral part of the study of religion, but it would also make an excellent topic for an integrated course. The pupils could look at man through the eyes of different disciplines—the sciences, the creative arts, etc.—as well as through the eyes of the major religions and non-religious systems of belief.

This kind of inter-disciplinary study serves to remind us that the usual grouping of R.E. with History, Geography and English under the heading 'Humanities' is far too restrictive. It was the natural result of assuming that religious education's main concern was human values. The recognition that R.E.'s task is much wider than this and that the study of religion is in itself a multi-disciplinary activity has opened the door to a wider and more interesting set of possibilities for integrated work. The unit 'Asking Questions' for instance depends on the comparison of quite distinct areas of human experience.

Religious education is certainly concerned with human values, but in the way described in chapters 4—7, with the intention of enabling pupils to explore and reflect upon human experience, rather than with the intention of shaping the pupils' own lives in a particular way.

At First school level it is the implicit element that is likely to be the main contribution of R.E. to integrated work, and even in the Middle school it will still be important in topic work. To check whether there is an R.E. contribution in a theme or a topic we shall ask whether it meets the criteria of helping the pupils to understand themselves, other people and the natural world better, whether it helps them to understand better their relationship to other people and to the natural world, and whether it raises for them questions about human experience and about the mystery of what it is to be human (see chapter 5). (Such an approach is, incidentally, likely to be more effective in the moral development of the pupils than a more direct linking of certain kinds of behaviour with biblical teaching.)

We have looked at a number of ways in which religious education can be integrated with other aspects of the curriculum. The fact that it is a multi-disciplinary subject with a complex structure means that the possibilities of integrating are almost infinite. But it also calls for both comprehensive understanding of the subject and very clear thinking about the best ways in which it can be integrated at different age and ability levels. This demands specialist knowledge at the Middle school stage and above, and at First and Junior school stage a resource person who can take special responsibility for keeping up to date with religious education, and who can therefore co-ordinate the subject in the school and act in an advisory capacity to the other teachers.

Without this specialist knowledge of the subject the attempt to integrate religious education is likely to be both confused and confusing.

18

Assuming the worst

'All this idealistic R.E. is fine, but it just wouldn't work in my situation.'
This could well be the reaction of a fair proportion of the teachers who
read this book. They have considerable sympathy with the fabled
Irishman who replied to a request for directions to a certain place, 'If
I were going there I wouldn't start from here'. The last chapter will
therefore deal specifically with two groups of problems which might
lie behind such a reaction.

The first group could be expressed like this:

'My pupils aren't bright enough. They just couldn't cope with the
range of material or the concepts involved in this kind of R.E.'
'I teach mixed ability classes. You couldn't teach most of these units
right across the ability range.'

The second group would be:

'If I could wipe the slate clean and start again I'd enjoy teaching this
kind of religious education, but there'd be chaos if I tried to take "Who
was Jesus?" with the fourth forms or "The Nature of Religious Language" with the fifths.'
'It's impossible in sixth form colleges becuase the students come
from a number of secondary schools and most of them are completely
anti-R.E. by the time we get them. They just don't want to hear.'

These two sets of problems are in one sense related, even though the
first refers to less able pupils and the second applies also to the most
academic ones. The key here lies in building up understanding. Although
the more academic pupils will be able to achieve this more rapidly, they
still need to have gained understanding in certain areas before they can
proceed to others.

However, before discussing what we do with the pupils whose previous
experience of R.E. makes it impossible to tackle the units suggested for
their age group, let us look at the problem of teaching the less able
pupils, both on their own and in mixed ability classes. The expression

'less able' is being used rather than 'slow learners' because there are some highly intelligent pupils who, for one reason or another, find learning a problem, but we are here thinking specifically of those pupils of Middle school age and above whose gifts do not lie on the intellectual side, who find conceptualisation difficult, who have little facility in the handling of language, and who find writing a laborious and unrewarding activity.

We have already said (p.18) that the kind of R.E. outlined in this book is intended for all the levels of ability to be found in the normal school system and that it is a fallacy to think that young people who aren't articulate about their thoughts and feelings are therefore not interested in serious topics or questions about the meaning of life. But they do require a different approach. The skill of the teacher of less able pupils will be shown in the breaking down of topics into small manageable units, in the structuring of these units in a logical order, in the presentation of abstract issues in concrete and personal terms, and in the emphasis put on the visual, on practical activities and on doing things carefully and thoroughly. Less able pupils are often expected to deal with topics at a superficial level on the assumption that they cannot go into things deeply. However, they are much less likely to take in anything that is being treated superficially. A remedial class of 11–12 year olds worked happily—and profitably—on 'Signs and Symbols' for six weeks. They started with road signs with which they were familiar. They went on to the signs they knew about in mathematics (which was a useful reinforcement), then the flags of several countries, including the composite Union Jack, and finally the Cross which they saw on the Christian Church. The emphasis at each stage was on the visual and the practical. In contrast to the conventional practice of introducing a topic in discussion and then in the second half of the lesson getting the pupils to do some written work or drawing, they were allowed to start by drawing. The discussion (which would be more accurately described as conversation) arose out of what they had produced. They were thus able to contribute something to the discussion and although it was on a limited scale it was good for their morale, and it helped in the learning process.

It is a sad reflection on our education system that most of the less able pupils leave school with no area of 'expertise'. They are at a disadvantage in any conversation because there is no field in which they are able to hold their own in any significant way. (The only exception for many of them is football, but it is not likely to be their class lessons which have given them the knowledge and the consequent confidence in this area.)

One of our concerns in religious education therefore will be to try to ensure that as a result of every unit we do our pupils—less able as well as academic—gain specific knowledge and understanding.

This is more likely to happen if they are involved in producing some kind of tangible end-product. Where R.E. lessons consist largely of 'talking', pupils not only get the impression that the subject is a soft option in which you don't have to work, but it means that they have to adopt a relatively passive role. In a class of thirty there is no time for many to speak more than once during the course of a lesson, i.e., apart from the teacher, who may not be able to resist the temptation to say something after each pupil's contribution. In addition, this very cerebral method of teaching makes learning especially problematic for those pupils who find conceptualisation difficult.

If the class is creating something tangible as the scheme proceeds they are actively involved in the work. They are having to think about the topic as they discuss how best to express what they are finding out. And the effect is cumulative. They have a constant reminder of what they did in earlier stages of the unit. Practical work can take many forms but we should not forget the value for less able pupils of making a tape, which extends considerably the possibilities for those for whom writing is slow and laborious.

Languages like Hebrew and Arabic are invaluable for slow learners. Because the alphabets are completely different from the English alphabet, and are more like drawing than writing, the pupils are not inhibited by any previous experience of failure. Encounter with such languages can also have an excellent effect on morale. One second year class who were acutely aware of being the 'bottom' stream in a secondary school spent a whole period of delighted concentration on the Hebrew alphabet—putting their names into Hebrew and learning the meaning of several familiar words, like Elijah. As they passed 2A on the stairs at the end of the period they said with tremendous pride, 'We've done Hebrew!' An activity which gives the less able pupils a sense of achievement and an interest in their lessons is not to be despised, but it can also have a positive value for R.E., particularly in units dealing with other religions. In addition to copying passages in the relevant language they should write underneath them the English translation, and provided the passages have been chosen carefully the knowledge of that religion is being extended without resort to the conventional methods of teaching which are so ineffective with the less academic pupils.

All this applies also to the less able pupils in mixed ability classes (though it is really only an indication of ways in which the learning process is helped, and the more academic pupils could also benefit from it). The key to mixed ability teaching, in religious education as in any other aspect of the curriculum, lies in individual and group work. There are occasions when it is right to deal with the class as a whole, but formal class lessons provide the least effective learning situation, and any teaching which aims at the middle of the ability range is doing a grave disservice to all the pupils on either side of that mid-point.

The use of group activities, or individual projects, is particularly important in the first year of a Middle, Secondary or Upper school if the pupils have come from a number of contributing schools where they have had different experiences of religious education. Repetition can be boring but taking knowledge and understanding further can be exciting. Only careful planning can ensure that the pupils who have already done something on a topic are allowed both to act as resource persons and contribute from their knowledge, and to take their study further than will be possible for those who are just beginning it.

In mixed ability classes the teacher's skill will be shown in the organisation of the work so that each group—and in fact each individual—has tasks that match its abilities and interests. However, a word of warning here. We have to structure group work so that it contributes to the pupils' understanding of the topic as a whole—so that we achieve the aim of the unit with all the pupils. It is only too easy for the teacher to have the complete picture and for the pupils not to be able to see how their section of the topic relates to the whole. To take the unit 'Masada' as an example, this could result if one group concentrated on the Roman army and another on the Zealot community. Some understanding of both sides is essential in this unit, but the activities relating to each of the sides must be varied enough to cater for the whole ability range.

There is nothing distinctive about mixed ability teaching within religious education; it merely requires the application of those principles and methods which are more usually applied in subjects like mathematics.

So far we have discussed method and general approach, but what about content? If we are going to tackle less material and deal with it more thoroughly we obviously have to select a limited number of units. What follows is a possible five year syllabus. It is designed with the less academic pupils in mind but the principles involved are those we need to apply in the area covered by the second group of problems. Teachers of more academic classes might well follow a similar syllabus if they face some of the same difficulties, especially lack of interest in the subject. The main differences will lie in the greater amount of material which can be included in individual units and in the opportunities for taking the study much further with the senior forms.

This syllabus assumes the worst:

One lesson a week.

The pupils have no initial interest in the subject.

The attitude of the school to religious education is negative.

In their primary schools the pupils did not have the kind of R.E. on which one can build satisfactorily in the secondary school.

The pupils will leave school as soon as they reach the statutory age.

Year	Autumn term	Spring term	Summer term
1	Masada	Creation Myths	Signs and Symbols
2	Festivals	How the Bible Came to Us	Barriers Mario Borrelli
3	Asking Questions	Sacred Writings	Fear Mother Teresa
4	What is Man?	What is Belief? Belief and Life	Who was Jesus?
5	Worship	Suffering	Hinduism & Sikhism

The units have been selected with three purposes in mind: to create interest and a positive attitude at an early stage; to build up understanding gradually; to include all the main elements that are necessary for an understanding of religion.

Only one unit has been suggested for most of the terms. This is to emphasise the importance of dealing with a topic thoroughly and giving pupils an opportunity to become 'experts' in each topic as the course proceeds. With only one period a week there is not a great deal of spare time in a term if the unit is to be tackled as a project rather than as a 'lecture course' delivered by the teacher interspersed with exercises in writing or drawing. However, there might well be three or four lessons at the end of a term even when a unit has been done thoroughly, and this provides an opportunity for other activities, such as reading sections of a book and discussing them (see chapter 7).

This selection of units is certainly not the only possible one for achieving the three purposes indicated, nor is it the only possible order, but it might be useful to explain why these particular units have been chosen.

'Masada' has been put first because the story of the defence of the rock fortress is dramatic; the account of the archaeological expedition in 1963–64 is fascinating, and the overwhelming response to an appeal for help which was coupled with a promise of hardship is right for this age group; there is plenty of scope for both practical and imaginative work which does not demand the ability to handle abstract thinking; it provides some background knowledge of the biblical period without any of the negative associations the pupils might have developed about Bible stories; it creates a way into the study of Judaism and it gives the pupils some insight into the spirit of modern Israel. In addition to all this it is one of the easiest of the units for a teacher to handle. It thus has all the ingredients for success—a most important factor for the beginning of a new syllabus.

'Creation Myths' has been put next because it provides a complete contrast in both content and way of working. This variety is important, partly to give freshness to the study and partly to help the pupils to realise something of the diversity of the subject. There are also advantages to be gained from doing 'Creation Myths' in the spring term when there is a visible reminder of the renewing of creation. However, if a class is so self-conscious about the creative activities suggested that it couldn't tackle them with any seriousness, then 'Signs and Symbols' would be a better unit to follow 'Masada' because it is a more matter of fact study, and 'Creation Myths' should be postponed until a more positive attitude has developed.

Looking at the units suggested for the first two years we see that the pupils would have encountered most of the aspects of religion. The implicit element—the exploration of and reflection upon human experience—would have come in 'Creation Myths', in 'Barriers' and in the story of Mario Borrelli. In this story they would also have thought about the relationship between belief and life—to be built on in the story of Mother Teresa in Year 3 and then looked at more systematically in Year 4. In 'Masada' they would have discovered that there are facts to be learned in the study of religion (not just beliefs to be argued about), and that the facts can help us to understand other people and the things that matter to them. In 'Signs and Symbols' they would have learned that some things point to a meaning beyond themselves—a necessary foundation for understanding that the rituals and ceremonies which are associated with festivals (Year 2) and worship (Year 5) have a deeper significance than appears on the surface. From 'Signs and Symbols' they would also realise that we use words (and non-verbal forms of communication) in different ways, and this would be built on later in 'Asking Questions' and 'What is Belief?'. In 'How the Bible Came to Us' they would be doing a factual study which is an essential pre-requisite both for looking at the wider field 'Sacred Writings' and for considering teachings from the Bible—which form a part of all but the last of the units in Years 4 and 5.

The syllabus ends with Hinduism and Sikhism for several reasons. The pupils who are going to leave school at the earliest possible moment are the ones who are most likely to resent a syllabus which comes to a climax with Christianity. They will have considered the Christian faith in one form or another in 13 of the units and they will have looked at most of its important aspects. Hindiusm and Sikhism have an appeal because they are Eastern religions, but there is positive value in studying religions which are practised by many people in Britain today. The emphasis should be on the way of life of a Hindu or a Sikh, rather than on belief systems, and if the pupils have followed this syllabus they should have a great deal to bring to their study of these religions in their fifth year.

This syllabus, like the complete chart of units, assumes that the pupils are starting at the beginning and working through. But what does one do with Year 2 and above when one first introduces such a syllabus? This will depend to a considerable extent on the school and the pupils but there are some units (or the ideas contained in them) which are essential for any understanding of religion and it will be no use trying to tackle later units before the pupils have had a chance to learn about them.

A possible plan for the first year of a new syllabus in a secondary school might look like this:

Year	Autumn term	Spring term	Summer term
1	Masada	Creation Myths	Signs and Symbols
2	Signs and Symbols Creation Myths	Festivals Mario Borrelli	How the Bible Came to Us Barriers
3	Signs and Symbols Myths	Festivals Mario Borelli	How the Bible Came to Us Fear
4	Festivals Symbols and Myths	How the Bible Came to Us Sacred Writings	Asking Questions Fear
5	Festivals Symbols and Myths	How the Bible Came to Us Sacred Writings	Asking Questions Fear

This plan has been suggested with the teacher in mind as well as the pupils. It is important that the teacher should start with a limited number of units (though this list is daunting enough) and should consolidate knowledge of both the material and of what the best learning experiences are for the pupils in relation to each unit. The units would need to be tackled in a different way with older pupils, and the actual decisions about content and method would be taken in the light of the intellectual and emotional stages of development of the pupils concerned.

The doubling up of units after Year 1 is not meant to suggest a superficial treatment. It is recognising that Year 2 and above are going to have less time to build up their understanding of religion and it will therefore be necessary to select the key areas and concepts in each unit for thorough study rather than try to cram the same amount of material into half the time. The important thing is that the material selected, and the work the pupils do on it, should enable the aim of the unit to be achieved for the whole class.

Shortage of time looms largest when a new approach to a subject is being introduced at sixth form level. It is virtually impossible to tackle adequately any of the units suggested for the fifteen-plus age group because they all depend on a considerable amount of prior factual knowledge and understanding. However, there are ways of making the best of a difficult situation.

One possibility would be to select units from those suggested for the previous age group, while handling them in such a way as to recognise the greater maturity of the sixth formers. In this case a possible order would be: 'Asking Questions', 'What is Man?', 'Sacred Writings', 'What is Belief?', 'Who was Jesus?'.

If the students were keen to discuss problems of philosophical theology such as miracle or the problem of evil, then it would be essential to precede such a discussion by 'Asking Questions' and 'What is Belief?'. If the unit 'Worship' were to be done, then the early part of it must include some elements from the units 'Sacred Places' and 'Festivals'.

It is always important to ask: What knowledge and understanding would the pupils have brought to a particular study if they had done the earlier units in the chart? and What are the key elements which this unit assumes and builds on, and which must therefore be included if it is to be adequately done? 'Asking Questions', for example, assumes some understanding of the fact that man uses language in different ways, and that he expresses what is significant in his experience in different ways (met particularly in 'Signs and Symbols', 'Creation Myths', 'Who am I?', 'Night and Day', 'Story of the Wise Men'). 'What is Man?' also assumes all this but in addition it assumes the questions about human experience raised by the human experience themes, plus the fact that celebration is a human characteristic, as is the association of special significance with certain places and events (met in 'Festivals', 'Sacred Places' and 'Signs and Symbols').

If world religions are to be studied by sixth formers who have not done the necessary earlier study, then it is essential that the scheme of work should include relevant sections of the units 'Sacred Places', 'Festivals', 'Sacred Writings' and 'Worship'—with the aim being to try to understand what it is like to be a Hindu, or a Muslim.

Our ultimate aim will be the same, whether we are able to build up a syllabus over a pupil's whole period of schooling or whether we have only one year before he leaves school, and that is to help him to understand the nature of religion and what it would mean to take a religion seriously.

CHART OF TEACHING UNITS

Aim: To help pupils to understand, by the time they leave secondary school, what religion is and what it would mean to take a religion seriously.

	Human experience themes	*Explicit – general*
5–7	Homes and Families Colours Babies Hands Parties	
7–9	Feet Our School Growing Up Night and Day	
9–11	Journeys Courage Sight Who am I?	Creation Myths Sacred Places
11–13	Barriers	Signs and Symbols Festivals
13–15	Fear What is Man?	Asking Questions Sacred Writings What is Belief? Belief and Life Judaism; Islam
15+	Conflict Suffering[1] Life after Death[1]	The Nature of Religious Language Worship Sikhism; Hinduism Buddhism The Study of Religion

[1] Includes explicit aspect

Explicit – Biblical and Christian	Biblical image themes	Biographies (examples)
Home Life of a Jewish Child at the Time of Jesus Synagogue School at the Time of Jesus Christmas–Santa Claus	Shepherd	
Life in Palestine in Bible Times Jesus–seen through Peter's eyes Archaeology Masada; Qumran; Solomon; Patriarchs How the Bible Came to Us	Bread Water	Father Damien James Evans Helen Keller Theodore Pennell
The Church in Action Coventry Cathedral; Christian Aid ... Christmas Customs Story of the Wise Men	Light	Anne Frank Mario Borrelli
The Bible in Christianity Who was Jesus?	Fire	Danilo Dolci Toyohiko Kagawa Mother Teresa Vinoba Bhave
Christian Life and Thought in 19th and 20th Centuries– Science and Religion; Rise of Biblical Criticism; the Church and the Churches; Christian Encounter with Other Faiths; the Church in a Technological Age; Experiments in Christian Community ... Problems in Philosophical Theology– existence of God; creation; evil; miracles; providence ...	Pilgrim People	Hannah Senesh Martin Luther King Mahatma Gandhi

Units

These notes are not intended as ready-made schemes of work. They are merely a guide. Teachers must adapt and select to suit their own situation.

There are a small number of units in which the material needs to be handled in a certain order because of the logical building up of concepts within the units, and these are marked *. Otherwise the starting point should be decided in the light of all the factors which only the teacher knows about in relation to a particular class.

The notes are in abbreviated form, and should be used in conjunction with the discussion of aims and general approach in the main part of the book.

Notes for units suggested for Upper school pupils tend to be more concentrated than those for younger pupils because teachers of the older age group should be R.E. specialists and therefore more at home in the subject. In addition, the thirteen-plus units require a great deal of knowledge on the part of the teacher, and the notes are merely pointers to the kind of knowledge and understanding which each unit demands.

The bibliography references at the end of some of the units are not meant to be a complete book list; they serve to draw attention to books whose titles might not indicate their relevance to the unit.

Human experience themes

(See chapters 4 and 5)
There are so many ways in which these themes might be tackled that the notes are merely indications of possible emphases and activities. Some of them will be suitable for one class or group of children and not for another. They are therefore pointers, not outline themes. Possible exceptions are 'Growing Up' and 'Who am I?' which are designed to achieve a specific aim.

142

5–7

Homes and families

Homes are more than houses and although the children can talk about and draw pictures of the actual building they live in, the emphasis should be on people, on belonging, sharing and interdependence, and on helping the child to be aware of his identity and place in the family—what he receives from the other members and what he has to give.

There are different kinds of 'families'. Children who come from one-parent families or who live in a children's home are still part of a family and should be encouraged to talk naturally about their family and their home.

It may be appropriate to have an imaginary family, either created by the class or 'adopted' from a story, to make a house for them, make up stories about their activities, have a birthday party for one of the children . . .

V A 14, 26.

Colours

Awareness and recognition of colours, especially in the world around.

Variations within one 'colour', e.g., green or blue. The effect of light and shade, texture . . .

Colour in nature: rocks, soils, plants, trees, birds, animals (including protective colouring). Changing colours: growing bulbs, new leaves, opening flowers . . . Colour in the seasons.

Colour in water: in different kinds of containers, in sunshine and shadow, pools and puddles, lakes, the sea. Oil on water. Blowing bubbles.

Colour in the sky: different blues, sunset, clouds . . .

Creating colours: mixing paints, tissue paper or cellophane against the windows. The rainbow. Spinning circle of rainbow colours to make white. Painting pictures to show colours.

Colours which tell us something: traffic lights, road markings, Red Cross, port and starboard lights . . .

Babies

This theme is particularly appropriate when the mother of one of the children is either expecting or has just given birth to a baby. Where this coincides with the period leading up to Christmas there is an added bonus.

Emphasis should be on preparations, excitement, joy, caring, and on the helplessness and dependence of babies.

Growth: need for sleep, certain kinds of food, security—physical support, cuddling . . .

How babies communicate with other people. How other people communicate with them.

Baby birds and animals. How they are cared for, fed, protected, taught to fend for themselves . . .

If the children can watch chicks hatching they will glimpse something of both the wonder of new life and the struggle and effort associated with birth.

V A 12, 17.

Hands

Skills children have been mastering: buttoning coats, tying knots, throwing and catching bean bags, painting, writing . . .

Creating with our hands: painting pictures, finger painting, clay modelling, making collages, making models, percussion music . . .

People who use their hands in their work: carpenters, cooks, cleaners, teachers, traffic wardens, mothers, gardeners . . .

People who use their hands to give pleasure to others: painters, sculptors, musicians . . .

Structure of the hand: what we can and can't do with our hands and fingers. Baby gripping. Span. Early measurements (and measuring the height of a horse today). Uniqueness of thumb print.

Actions with hands: shaking hands, stroking, pulling, hitting, poking, supporting . . .

How hands 'talk': waving, clapping, beckoning, threatening, pointing . .

Parties

Emphasis on celebration, being happy, taking trouble, making other people happy.

Birthday parties, Christmas parties, family reunion parties . . .

Find an occasion to have a class party. (See the end of 'Homes and Families'.) Children make list of all the things to be done. Make and send out invitations—possibly including caretaker, crossing patrol, parson . . .

Make decorations, possibly on the theme of 'things which make us happy'.

Prepare food: sandwiches with cress grown in the classroom, simple cakes or sweets made by the children . . .

Clearing up after the party . . .

7–9

Feet

The approach could be similar to that suggested for 'Hands', though it would be geared to a slightly older age group and would include skipping, hop-scotch, football, dancing . . . People who have no hands and who have to use their feet for writing or typing . . .

Compare human feet and the feet of animals and birds: footprints, different functions of feet—climbing, digging, balancing on perches or branches . . .

Our school

Construction and layout. Number of rooms, measurements. If the school has been recently built, look at the plans. Visit a local building site to find out about foundations, building materials.

The school as a community: the work of the head, teachers, caretaker, kitchen helpers, crossing patrol, pupils . . . Emphasis on the work not seen by the children—caretaker's hours, teachers' work before and after school. Activities of the community—assembly, concerts, helping in the neighbourhood . . .

People who visit the school: suppliers, school meals delivery men, medical staff, groundsmen, parents . . .

How are visitors, new pupils, new teachers, etc., made welcome in the school?

The school and the neighbourhood: catchment area, children's journeys to school, shops children use, teachers' centre (teachers also learn!) . . .

The school in the past. Use elderly people (especially lonely ones) as resource persons, to find out what school was like when they were young and what changes there have been. V A 24.

Growing up

The aim is to help the children to explore and reflect upon the factors involved in growing up, particularly change and development, and dependence on other people.

Make a study of young children, i.e., up to five or six years. Children use their own younger brothers and sisters or 'adopt' some for the purpose of the study. Keep records of the children being studied and show these on charts.

Physical development. What babies and young children can do at different ages, e.g., sitting up, standing, walking, what they can do with their hands ... List things a baby, a three year old, a six year old could not do if alone in a house. Observe babies learning to walk, discuss the best way of helping. What kind of encouragement does one give?

Growth of language. How babies and young children communicate with other people at different ages. The importance of non-verbal communication. At home the children observe their 'sample' and write down (if they can cope with writing) how babies and young children ask for what they want. N.B. 7—9 year olds need precise—and limited— tasks, e.g., five minutes' observation at the beginning of a meal time, repeated on a number of days. Build up chart from the children's obser- vation of how children use words at different stages, e.g., starting with words like Mummy and Daddy, naming objects, then adding verbs, then constructing sentences. How does one help a baby to learn to talk? How would we learn if we grew up without other human beings?

Emotional development. Find out what makes babies and young children at different ages happy, frustrated, frightened, confident . . . How do they express these feelings? What kinds of games do children like to play at different ages? Notice the growing importance of having friends to play with.

A study of animals growing up could be done alongside the human study. The different ways in which animals and birds care for their young. How the young are prepared for adult life—play, etc. Children show on a block graph the comparative length of childhood of humans and certain birds and animals.

Night and day

Emphasis on helping children to understand the rhythms of the natural world, to appreciate the positive value of night, and to come to terms with their own fears of the dark.

Plants' need for light—grow cress in the light, in the dark and in a three-sided box. Plants which close up at night, or which are night-scented.

Nocturnal animals and birds.

People who work at night: in hospitals, transport, P.O., shift workers . . .

Keep daily diaries—pattern of night and day activities. Compare children's and adults' patterns. Man's need for sleep.

Measurement of time. Twenty-four hour clocks.

Seasonal changes. Show lengthening (or shortening) days on a graph. Compare polar and equatorial regions. Reason for alternation of night and day and for seasonal variations. Time zones.

Man's fascination with the sun and the moon. Ancient cosmologies. Myths.

This theme lends itself particularly to visual presentation and to poetry writing.

9–11

Journeys
Emphasis should be on interdependence, expectation, going into the unknown.

Comparison of familiar daily journeys with occasional journeys—day trips, longer holidays, school journey. Aim, expectation, preparations. On a particular journey—what activities? what learnt? what things went wrong? Are we any different as a result of our journeys?

People whose work is travelling: sailors, train and bus drivers, pilots . . . Journeys made to help people: ambulance, fire brigade, lifeboat team . . . Individuals or groups might make a detailed study of one of the above, to try to enter into the actual life.

Journeys of exploration, e.g., Scott, Hunt and Hillary, Thor Heyerdahl . . .

Space travel, e.g., one of the Apollo missions. Emphasis on the human element: preparations, teamwork, vast number of people involved in mission and sharing responsibility for its success.

Lone journeys, e.g., single-handed trans-Atlantic, or round the world. What, apart from physical dangers, would such voyagers have to face?

The theme of the journey and the quest in literature.

Possibly a study of the migration patterns of certain birds and animals. Emphasis on timing, distances covered, routes, hardships faced, and the 'miracle' of unaccompanied migrations of the young of some species. V A 37, 63, 68; V B 12.

Courage

Different kinds of courage:

Physical bravery—in war, in natural disasters, against the elements, in situations of danger (e.g., Pennell).

People who show courage for the sake of others: mountain rescue teams, lifeboatmen; people who give one of their kidneys; Fr. Damien, Mother Maria. Discuss what makes people sacrifice themselves or risk danger for others.

Showing courage in everyday life. Possibly writing on 'The day I showed courage'.

The courage of people who face and overcome hardships and handicaps—bereavement, physical handicap (e.g., Helen Keller).

Moral courage. In what ways is this different from physical courage?

This theme is best tackled through biographies and literature so that the pupils can 'get inside' situations and appreciate the nature of the courage shown. Most of the books in V A 47—69 could be used, but especially 51, 58, 61, 64, 66, 67, 68. Also V B 25, 27.

Sight

Structure of the eye: human eye compared with eye of fly, bird of prey . . . Long and short sight. Work of opticians.

Colour vision. Contrast other animals except higher primates.

Extension of sight: magnifying glass, microscope, telescope, periscope . . .

Photography: how the camera 'sees' . . .

Deceiving our eyes: optical illusions, mirages, conjuring . . .

Blindness: link with other senses, Braille, Helen Keller, guide dogs, talking books . . .

Extension of the use of language about sight: meaning of 'I see', insight, foresight, mind's eye, vision . . .

Who am I?

This unit has been designed as a sequel to 'Growing Up'. If the children have not done 'Growing Up' the aims and some of the material will need to be incorporated in this unit.

The aim is to help the children, through an exploration of physiology and elementary psychology, to realise the complexity and wonder of human beings, and to consider the nature of continuity and change in a human person.

Physiology:

A study of the human body, e.g., the way the skeleton is held together, the percentage of the body that is water, how muscles work, the work of the nervous system in receiving and transmitting 'messages' . . .

A more detailed study of the eye, or the ear, or the respiratory system . . . (See notes on 'Sight'.)

Children collect photos of themselves at different ages and consider differences and similarities between babyhood and now.

Find out period of renewal of different parts of the human body—bloodstream, cells, hair, nails . . . The human body is completely renewed physically in a period of seven years. Children consider in what sense they are the same person they were seven years ago.

Psychology:

This is best done by a study of younger brothers and sisters. (See 'Growing Up'.) Observations can be more rigorous and more sustained than was possible with younger pupils and the age group studied can be extended to about two years younger than the age of the class. It may be possible to tape young children's conversation.

Find out main interests of children at different ages—TV programmes, stories, games . . .

In what ways does the relationship with adults and with other children change between birth and nine years?

What things make babies and young children happy, frustrated, frightened . . . at different ages?

If the children have changed so much already, in what sense are they the same person? Will they change in the future? Will they still be the same person at thirteen or eighteen or when they are as old as their parents or grandparents are now?

11–13

Barriers

Different kinds of barriers. Are all barriers bad?

Physical barriers—man-made and natural: crush barriers, road blocks, fire guards, prison walls, mountains, sea, national frontiers . . .

Barriers to understanding. Main areas of misunderstanding:

Age—young children and older brothers and sisters, teenagers and parents . . .

Sex—Are there intellectual or emotional differences between boys and girls? Meaning of the 'weaker sex'? In what ways is it easier to be a boy? a girl? What makes relationships between the sexes easy? difficult?

Language—foreign languages, regional accents, regional or national words and expressions, e.g., for food, alleys . . . Words can mean different things to different people, e.g., children interpreting in the light of their experience, the same soldiers being called 'freedom fighters' and 'terrorists'. Why are words not precise instruments of communication?

Ignorance—of a person's motives, of previous events, of factual inform-ation, e.g., about the biology of race. Will the removal of ignorance stop a person being prejudiced? What other factors cause prejudice?

Minority groups—Asians and West Indians in Britain, English (or Scots) in other countries. Problems of retaining culture and identity, and assimilation to the culture of the host country.

How can the wrong kinds of barriers be broken down? Do all people agree about which are good barriers and which are bad?

IV 1, V A 48, 51, 56, 59, 61, 74, 79, 80.

Fear

Exploration of the idea of fear as a natural aspect of human experience.

Possible fears of different people: small children, old people, teen-agers, the unemployed, strangers, lone sailors . . .

Recognition of the necessity and value of some fears, e.g., for the survival of the species.

What makes some people afraid of darkness, physical danger, the unknown, loneliness, rejection, death . . . Are some fears rational and others irrational? Why are some people afraid of spiders and not of the dark and others afraid of the dark and not of spiders?

Possible ways of minimising fear—our own and other people's.

The relationship between fear and courage. A person with no fear shows no courage.
V A 66, 68, 88, 91, 94. Anne Frank.

What is man?
A study of the questions about man raised by the natural and behavioural sciences, and of the answers suggested to the question 'What is man?' by the major religions and non-religious systems of belief.

Man the animal—characteristics and limitations. Comparison with the rest of the animal kingdom.

Physical: agility, speed, motor control, anatomy. Perhaps detailed work on one aspect.

Psychological: fears, gregariousness, aggressiveness, aspirations, capacity for self-sacrifice . . .

Aesthetic: appreciation of beauty, ability to create works of art . . .

Intellectual: ability to communicate across time and space, to reflect on the past and plan for the future, to create—and adapt—moral codes, to interpret experience, to ask questions about meaning, to construct religious and ideological systems.

The nature and destiny of man as seen by such religious and ideological systems. (See p.62.) The concept of person, man's relationship to his fellows and to the natural world, his understanding of salvation. This study should include the rites of passage—birth, initiation, marriage, death—worship, festivals, social institutions, etc. It should not be concerned only with intellectual beliefs.
I A 23; V A 84. See also *Your Attention Please* by Peter Porter.

15+

Conflict
Main areas of human conflict. What do one day's newspapers reveal?

Take one particular example of conflict (or groups each take one): parents and teenagers, a local controversy, a current debate about the education system, Ulster, the Middle East . . . Find out all the arguments on both sides. Are there more than two sides? What events led up to the present conflict? How far back can one trace them? How complex are the reasons—personal, economic, racial, religious, political, historical . . .

Is conflict always bad? Can it be constructive? Is it necessary for progress? for creativity?

Compare conflict and aggression in man and in other species.

Is war inevitable? Why is it often glorified? What benefits have wars brought? Could they have been obtained in any other way?

Conflict between supporters of rival teams. Is it natural? What forms does it take?

Conflict between individuals—in families, at work, neighbours . . . Why does conflict between groups tend to become violent more easily than conflict between individuals?

Conflict within a person. Is an integrated person one who has no inner conflict? Is a person who accepts a set of beliefs, e.g., religious or political, likely to find less or more conflict, both within himself and with his fellows?

Look at the teaching of religions and non-religious systems of belief about peace, brotherhood, love, inoffensiveness, reconciliation, serenity, self-sacrifice . . . Why is it so difficult for men to live up to these beliefs? V A 84, 85, 86, 91, 99, 105. Martin Luther King, Gandhi.

Suffering
Similar approach to 'What is Man?'. An examination of the problem of suffering, especially the suffering of the innocent, and the answers suggested by some of the major religions and non-religious systems of belief to the questions 'What is the cause of suffering?', 'How do I come to terms with it?'

Different kinds of suffering: natural disaster, war, starvation, illness, bereavement, rejection, injustice . . .

Exploration of the protests against suffering: in literature—Job, some of the Psalms, war poetry . . .; in political and social action—Danilo Dolci, Mother Teresa, Sally Trench, Martin Luther King, Shelter, Christian Aid . . .; pacifism . . .

More detailed study of beliefs about and attitudes to suffering in Buddhism, Humanism, Christianity. Jewish suffering through history, and modern Jewish interpretation of suffering.

Expression of the answers to the problem of suffering as well as its analysis should involve poetry, the visual arts, and if possible music and dance.

Life after death

Man's perennial fascination with the question of life after death. Contemporary manifestations: spiritualism, interest in re-incarnation . . .

The ancient world: archaeological discoveries of burials, the river Styx and Hades in Greek thought, Sheol in Hebrew thought, development of belief in a resurrection in late biblical Judaism, early Christian beliefs about general resurrection and the resurrection of Jesus.

The beliefs of the major religions today: concepts of judgment, karma, nirvana, reincarnation, heaven . . . These should be studied through burial rites and customs as well as through formulated beliefs.

Explicit—general

9—13

Creation myths

The aim is to enable the pupils to discover, through the exploration of a number of creation myths, one of the ways in which man expressed what was significant in his experience.

Select at least three myths. Stories should be read to the whole class even when groups of children work on one story each.

Explore the myths by means of the expressive arts and work towards a presentation of the myths, through dance, with the children making up music (percussion), and making masks to show in symbolic form what they are representing.

Pupils look for the main motifs in each myth. How many of them appear in more than one myth? Conflict—chaos and order, light and dark, good and evil, obedience and rebellion. Fantasy in sizes and proportions—a body or a tree filling the sky, an egg yolk becoming the sun. Struggle and effort—superhuman tasks to be accomplished. Consciousness that something has gone wrong in the world—original intention good. The need for sacrifice, sometimes self-sacrifice, as the only way to accomplish some purpose.

Use of creative writing, especially poetry, painting, etc., to express the motifs of the myths.

Find out about the place of origin of the myths, to understand why, e.g., some speak of land coming up out of the sea (Finnish, Gilbertese) and others of primordial ice (Norse).

N.B. The creation stories in Genesis 1 and 2 can be used, but they are not primitive Hebrew myths. The Hebrews adapted myths from other lands in the Near East in order to express through them their own beliefs about God, his purpose for and his relationship with the natural world and man.

V B 5, 6, 10, 11, 13, 16, 21, 23.

Sacred places (see chapters 8 and 9)

The aim is to give the pupils factual information about the buildings used for worship in the main religions, to help them to see that all religions have sacred places, to let them discover that it is a human characteristic to have 'sacred' places.

Look at slides or pictures of typical buildings used for worship or meditation in different religions.

With the aid of reference books pupils produce pictures of exteriors, ground plans and interiors, illustrating significant features, e.g., mosque: mihrab, lectern, minaret, Qur'anic texts; synagogue: ark, bima, representations of menorah, letters of Divine Name; church: cross, communion table, Bible, font; gurdwara: langar, platform, canopy, Granth, pictures of the Gurus; Hindu temple: images and symbols of the gods, flowers, incense; Buddhist temple: images of the Buddha, flowers, incense.

Visit a local church, and places of worship of other faiths if there are any in the locality.

Ways in which the buildings are used in the different religions. Patterns of worship, use of the scriptures. Private prayer or meditation in the home. Shrines in the home (especially Hinduism).

Places of pilgrimage in the main religions. Why are these places important? Is it only religious people who visit them? Are there places of pilgrimage in the locality?

Other places which people visit because they have important associations—birthplace of a famous person, site of events in history, archaeological sites . . . In what ways are football grounds (or other sports grounds) similar to religious places of pilgrimage?

The BBC Radiovision series 'Encounter with' was prepared for sixth forms but many of the frames can be used to illustrate places of worship.

Signs and symbols*

The aim is to help the pupils to understand that signs and symbols are a
shorthand form of communication, that they convey more than they
actually 'say', but only to those who already know the 'language'. (There
are different theories about the distinction between a sign and a symbol
but this kind of discussion belongs at the Upper school level.)

Road signs. Select five or six; what might a visitor from China think
they stood for?

Trade marks . . . Make list from kitchen cupboard, TV commercials,
shops . . . Which ones bear some relationship to the product?

Signs in mathematics, both traditional and new. Include some of the
Greek letters. What does + stand for: plus? cross roads? positive
terminal? Red Cross?

Codes—intended to convey a message only to selected people. Often
used in times of persecution, cf. the Christian sign of the fish.

Letters of the alphabet stand for different sounds. Compare equivalent
sounds in English, Greek and Hebrew (esp. d, h, l, n, p, r, o).

Words used metaphorically. Make lists of expressions which are not
meant to be taken literally, e.g., night fell, he lost his head . . . Words
used symbolically in the Bible, e.g., cloud (the glory and presence of
God) and angel (messenger). Cloud: Ex. 13:21, 19:9,16, 24:15–18.
1 K. 8:6, 10–11, Mt. 17:5, Acts 1:9. Angel: Gen. 28:12, Mt. 2:13, 19,
Lk. 1:26f, 2:9, 13, Acts 5:19. Cf. the name of the fifth century B.C.
prophet Malachi—'my messenger'—'my angel'.

Many symbols are felt to be in some way more than just a sign. Compare the way people react if someone destroys a photo of a person who
is important to them. If someone burns or tramples on a flag it is felt
to be more than spoiling a piece of cloth; it is an action against the
nation itself.

Symbols used in religions. Compare the Red Cross being called the
Red Star of David in Israel and the Red Crescent in Muslim countries.
Why would the Jews and Muslims not want to use the cross as a symbol?

N.B. Other areas which can be included where appropriate: traffic lights
and railway signals, music notation, uniforms and badges, flags, Olympic
and Commonwealth symbols, fables, non-verbal signs (greetings, gestures,
etc.).
I A 19, 32; III 6, 9, 12; V A 63.

Festivals (see chapters 10 and 11)
The realisation that man is a celebrating animal. A study of both 'secular' and 'religious' celebration.

Family celebrations: birth, birthdays, weddings, Bar Mitzvah, anniversaries.

Celebrations in the local community: carnivals, sports team victories . .

National celebrations: Guy Fawkes, Hallowe'en, Remembrance Sunday, St. David's Day, New Year, May Day, Christmas . . . How does one draw a line between 'secular' and 'religious' celebration?

Main characteristics of celebrations: coming together, eating . . .

The different reasons for celebrating: new beginnings, success, deliverance, national or group solidarity . . . Are there dangers in any of our celebrations?

Exploration of some of the festivals of the major religions. Emphasis on how the festivals are celebrated today, and what the festivals are like for an adherent of the faith. Possible groupings are:
Festivals of light in the autumn term—Divali, Birthday of Guru Nanak, Chanukah, Christmas. New Year festivals—The First Muharram, Baisakhi, Rosh Hashanah, Advent. Spring festivals—Holi, Passover, Easter (especially in the Orthodox Church). Harvest festivals—Succoth, Harvest Thanksgiving. Celebrations associated with initiation rites—The Sacred Thread ceremony, Bar Mitzvah, Baptism.

The study of Christmas can be extended to include units under 'Biblical and Christian'.
I A 10, C 16, D 13, F 25.

13–15

Asking questions*
Exploration of the different kinds of questions man asks and the methods used to discover the answers.
Empirical questions:

a) Knowledge anyone can check—measurement, railway timetable . . .
b) (i) Questions which need specialist knowledge—Physics . . .
   (ii) Questions most of us will never be able to answer—how to put a space station into orbit . . .
c) Knowledge we can't be sure of in advance—the effects of certain drugs, how people will react in certain situations . . .

156

Experiments with testing by means of the senses, including the possibility of fooling our senses—use of familiar sounds which are difficult to identify, optical illusions, conjuring . . .

Aesthetic questions. Start with questions with reasonable consensus of opinion—how a poet or composer creates a certain effect. Move on to what a musician or artist was trying to convey. Does our understanding of the work depend on knowing the original intention? What makes a work of art 'good' or 'bad'?

Moral questions. Why do we call some actions 'good' and some 'bad'? Compare use of 'good' and 'bad' in aesthetics. Why is a particular action right in one society and wrong in another, right at one period, wrong in another?

How does one know what is the 'right' thing to do when faced with two courses of action which are both good—conflict of loyalties, or both bad—injuring one person or failing to protect another?

Ultimate questions. Is there a God? Is there life after death? Is there any meaning in life? . . . Why do people continue to ask these questions?

What kind of evidence counts in finding answers to the different kinds of questions? How far can the methods appropriate to one kind of question be used in seeking answers to another?

Does it matter equally if we can't be certain of the answers in the different areas? In what ways does knowing (or not knowing) the answers in each area affect our lives?

N.B. In religion there are different kinds of questions, not only ultimate ones. Empirical—What do we know about the life of Jesus or the Buddha? What is the origin of a particular festival? . . .Psychological—What is faith? . . . Ethical—What are the implications of a religious belief for the way one ought to live? . . . Many of the books in I G (c).

Sacred writings (see chapters 12 and 13)

The place of sacred writings in the major living religions. Include the form of the writings, the language and the type of literature.

Origin and growth, Muslim: Qur'an—through Muhammad, short period. Hadith longer period.

Hindu: Vedas, Upanishads, Bhagavad-Gita . . . Distinction between sruti and smriti. Variety—saga, philosophy, poetry . . . Written over a period of 1,000 years. Different beliefs in different writings.

Buddhist: Theravada–Tipitaka. Mahayana–Questions of King Milinda . . . Much Mahayana Buddhist literature dates from the N.T. period.

Sikh: Granth–collection of hymns and poems from the period of the Ten Gurus. Includes poems by Muslims and Hindus.

Jewish: (much greater detail) Only sacred writings to include the history of the people. Written over a period of 1,000 years. Variety– law, poetry, saga, prophetic oracles, different types of history . . . Editings. Sections of the Canon. Talmud–Rabbinic teachings, interpretations, stories . . . Developed over several centuries at beginning of Common Era.

Christian: (also in greater detail) Took over the Jewish Bible. Septuagint. Haphazard growth of N.T.–letters to young Churches, Gospels . . . Non-canonical writings–Shepherd of Hermas, Epistle of Barnabas, Didache . . . Apocryphal N.T. writings. Fixing of the Canon. *Authority*. Muslim: Qur'an God's final revelation of his nature and will. Holds the same place in Islam that Christ does in Christianity.

Hindu and Mahayana Buddhist writings not regarded as standards of orthodoxy. Compare Theravada attitude to the Tipitaka.

Sikhism: Granth called 'Guru Granth' because it contains the teaching of the ten Gurus and is the Sikhs' continuing teacher.

Jewish: growth of the Oral Law. Role of the Talmud in guidance for life. Place of the study of the Law in the Rabbinic period and today.

Christian: ambivalent position of the Scriptures–Word of God, not 'words' of God (cf. Muslim attitude to the Qur'an). Christians look for guidance to both the Scriptures and the living Spirit of God, therefore tension.

Look at Muslim attitude to Jews and Christians–'People of the Book', and biblical material in the Qur'an. Also Jewish attitude to the Christian handling of their Scriptures.

N.B. See also 'The Bible in Christianity'.   I A 33–36, C 4, D 5, 6, F 25.

What is belief?*
Exploration of the different ways in which we use the word 'belief'. (This unit builds on 'Asking Questions'.)
a) Beliefs that can be verified by checking–'that the last bus goes at 11.00 pm' . . .
b) Beliefs about a person's character (i) that can be verified in time–

'that if I lend him a book he will return it at the time promised' . . .
(ii) that can't be proved until the person is dead—'that he will never
let me down' . . . What are the grounds for trusting a person?

c) Beliefs that certain courses of action will produce certain results—
'that banning TV advertising of cigarettes will reduce smoking', 'that
raising the school leaving age will (will not) improve the quality of
our education system'. We have to act on our beliefs—and discover
later whether they had any foundation.

d) Beliefs that can't be proved or disproved—the existence of God, life
after death, that generosity is better than selfishness (or vice versa),
that Jesus is the Word of God, that the Qur'an is the Word of God . . .

The function of belief systems, religious and non-religious. N.B. In
the realm of ultimate questions everyone is a 'believer'. The atheist
believes that there is no God and no life after death, the Jew, Christian
and Muslim believe that there are.

The coherence of belief systems—why can't we just select some
beliefs from all the religions?   I A 1, G (c) 2, 26, 28, 33.

Belief and life*
A study of selected beliefs, especially about God and man, of the major
religions and humanism, and their implications for the life of the person
who holds them. This must be done in two stages:

1. Unpacking the belief, e.g., finding out what Christians mean when
they say that God became man, or what Buddhists mean when they
say that there is no such thing as the self. This task is not to be
undertaken lightly. The teacher must know a great deal about the
origin, and possible development, of the belief being studied, and its
relationship to the belief system as a whole.

2. Exploring what might be the implications for a Christian of the
belief that God became man, etc. A number of topics could be used
for such an exploration—personal relationships, community life,
race relations . . . Pollution, man's use of natural resources, etc.,
could be topics for exploring the implications of the Christian (and
Jewish and Muslim) belief that God is Creator.

It is best to concentrate on one or two beliefs and deal with them
thoroughly rather than attempt a superficial treatment of several. The
pupils as well as the teacher will need to learn about the language and

thought-forms of the period when the belief was formulated, and try to discover what those who originally formulated the belief wanted to say through it—and what they wanted to deny.

Judaism; Islam (see chapters 8, 9, 10 and 12)
The notes that follow apply to the teaching of any religion as a whole. Two religions have been put on the same line to indicate that either one or both might be taught to this age group.

Begin with what it means to be an adherent today, and distinguish between living in a country where the religion is the predominant faith and being in a minority group in an alien culture.

Focus on the family—growing up in a religion, especially initiation rites. Everyday life for the layman. Life for the member of a religious order (especially in Buddhism).

Worship and/or meditation, both communal and private. Place of the scriptures in worship or personal devotions.

Sacred places—buildings for worship, etc., shrines (including in the home), places of pilgrimage. Festivals. Nature, authority and use of sacred writings.

Founder (if appropriate), including cultural and religious background. Continuity and discontinuity with the religion out of which it emerged.

Any significant developments in history (founding of the Khalsa in Sikhism, the Hijra in Islam, Buddhism under Asoka, reform movements in Hinduism . . .) Major divisions within the religion—differences in geographical or cultural background, in beliefs, in practices . . .

The study of a religion should not be just learning about origins, main beliefs and practices. It should be an imaginative attempt to understand how the religion looks—and feels—to its adherents.

15+

The nature of religious language
This unit assumes the prior study of 'Signs and Symbols', 'Asking Questions' and 'What is Belief?'. If they have not been done then the key ideas from them should come at an early stage in this study.

Different ways in which we use language—sciences, ethics, poetry, metaphor . . .

Distinguish between the use of language in the study of religion and the use of language within a religion, e.g., language a Christian would use about God in credal statements or worship.

Analytical philosophy—the development from logical positivism to a recognition of the significance of language within its own discourse of meaning. Language games. How far is religious language an attempt to say something about reality? If it is, can it be understood only within the religious discourse of meaning?

Examine discussions of the problem of religious language—Ian Ramsey, John Macquarrie ...

See notes on 'Problems in Philosophical Theology' for the general approach to the study. I G (c) 9, 24, 25.

Worship (see chapter 15)
Understanding of a central dimension in man's religious experience.

Exploration of the different ways in which man expresses his compulsion to worship—secular as well as religious.

If the pupils have not studied 'Sacred Places', include examination of buildings used for worship in the major religions—similarities and differences.

Different ways of worshipping: in the home, individual prayers (especially Judaism and Islam), congregational worship, meditation ... Special occasions: festivals, pilgrimages.

More detailed study of Jewish and Christian worship, now and in biblical times. Christian worship's debt to Judaism.
N.B. Pupils should have an opportunity to experience the forms of worship they are studying, preferably by attending an act of worship of a religious community.

Sikhism; Hinduism; Buddhism
See notes under 'Judaism; Islam'.

The study of religion (see chapter 2 and p.61)
This unit should not be undertaken lightly. It needs a great deal of skill and specialist knowledge on the part of the teacher, and it presupposes considerable prior study on the part of the pupils both of the different

aspects of religion and of the ultimate questions which man asks about his existence.

The aim is to give the pupils some insight into the contemporary concerns of the study of religion, e.g., questions of reductionism, relativism and the sociology of knowledge. Sixth form pupils may well be interested in such questions as: Can religion be defined? What is the function of religion? Can religion be adequately explained in terms of the human sciences? Is religion entirely the product of social forces? . . .

If the pupils are to discuss these questions profitably, however, they will need some background knowledge of the study of religion in the past century. This should not be a solid historical study, but should seek to illustrate both the aims and the presuppositions of the key movements and figures:

The rise of the history of religions school

The foundations of anthropological study—Tylor, Frazer . . .

The foundations of sociological study—Robertson Smith, Durkheim . . .

The foundations of psychological study—Freud, Jung . . .

I A 1, 2, 28, 29, 38.

Explicit—biblical and Christian

7—9

Home life of a Jewish child at the time of Jesus (see pp.92, 101)
Food, clothes, structure of house, etc., should be included but much more important is what the life of the family would have been like. Close-knit family relationships; boy helping his father, especially at his trade which he would probably follow; girl helping her mother—fetching water, grinding corn, baking bread (daily), sweeping, sewing . . .

The work of the farmer—to be developed further in 'Bread' (see p.173)

The family going together to the synagogue on the Sabbath.

Synagogue school on weekdays for boys from the age of six. Learning Hebrew. Pupils make scrolls and copy Hebrew words.

Stories from the Scriptures told to the children. Possible examples for the pupils: David and Goliath (1 Sam. 17), Jeremiah being rescued from the well (Jer. 38), Moses' childhood in the court of the Pharaoh.

Visit to the Temple in Jerusalem in the spring for the Feast of the Passover, probably seeing shepherds and their flocks on the journey.

Pupils learn Ps. 122:1—2 (one of the pilgrim songs). Preparations for the Passover. Family Passover meal—role of the youngest son.

Reference to Jewish boys' and girls' family life today—synagogue, Bible, Passover, but above all the closeness of the family and the things they do together. I F 23, 27, G (b) 10, 12, 15, 19, 24.

Synagogue school at the time of Jesus (see p.83)
This unit should build on rather than repeat material in 'Home Life of a Jewish Child at the Time of Jesus'.

Synagogue school—House of the Book—for all boys from the age of six. They learned to read and write Hebrew. (They spoke Aramaic at home and probably learnt Greek as they grew up.) Let pupils 'play' with the Hebrew alphabet. (In Talmudic times children learnt the alphabet with letters covered with honey, and ate the honey after playing with the letters.)

Hebrew written from right to left, no capital letters, no vowels written, no spaces between the words and no punctuation. Pupils make scrolls and write out Ps. 23 with no capitals, vowels, spaces or punctuation. Copy first two verses of Ps. 23 in Hebrew, with modern spacing. (A local parson may have a Hebrew Bible if there is no Jewish person who could provide the quotation.)

The Shema (Dt. 6:4—5) was the first part of the Bible which the Jewish child learnt to recite. Much of the boys' study would be of the Bible (i.e. the Christian Old Testament). Many different kinds of writing:

Poetry—Ps. 23, Ps. 150. Compare poetry and prose descriptions in English writings.

Stories about heroes of the past—David, Gideon (Jg. 6f.). Compare Alfred the Great, Drake . . . The development of stories about them which tell us something about the hero's character. Cf. David and Goliath.

Stories with a plot, more like a short novel—Joseph (Gen. 37—47).

Different kinds of laws—laws made long before when the people of Israel stopped being nomads and became farmers (Dt. 25:4, 19:14), and laws about how to keep the Sabbath as a very special day.

Older Juniors might include the teachings of the prophets—Amos and his concern for social justice, attacking market traders who rigged their scales (Amos 8:5) and rich people who didn't care about the poor (6:4—6).

Pupils should get a clear idea of the different kinds of writing through learning about the different situations for which they were produced.
I G (b) 10, 13, 15, 17, 22.

Christmas—Santa Claus

The aim is to help the children to discover the many ways in which the figure of Santa Claus is represented in different countries, and to recognise that the same theme—generous and often anonymous giving—underlies the variations.

The story of the original Santa Claus—St. Nicholas, the Archbishop of Myra in Asia Minor.

Children work in groups, each group 'adopting' one country (or two) and finding out as much as possible about the form in which Santa Claus is looked for—the Lucia Bride in Sweden, the Three Kings in Spain, the Christ Child in Austria . . .

The results can be shown on a large frieze. The groups can dress up and act out the customs of their 'adopted' country for the rest of the class or in assembly. N.B. The Rolf Harris song 'The Six White Boomers' tells of the year that Santa 'did a double run' across Australia to return a lost joey (baby kangaroo) to its mother. It is on the record 'Mary's Boy Child' (IE 162 91922).
I G (a) 33.

9–13

Life in Palestine in Bible times

If pupils are doing biblical image themes, this study should be about life in Galilee or Jerusalem at the time of Jesus rather than about early times. It should build on 'Home Life of a Jewish Child' and 'Synagogue School', extending rather than repeating. Pupils can now make a much more detailed study of the synagogue, the Temple, the festivals . . . The study should be taken from the point of view of Judaism, and source material which presents Jewish practices and attitudes in a negative light should be avoided.

Pupils should be helped to recognise aspects of Jewish life which are different today.

Jesus—seen through Peter's eyes (see chapter 14)
The approach suggested for this kind of unit is outlined on p.102.

Pupils can pretend to be Peter and keep diary accounts of their experiences.
I G (a) 1, 40.

Archaeology—Masada
Yigael Yadin's appeal for help and promise of hardship. World-wide response.

The archaeological expedition: preparation, work of the volunteers, work of the scientific team, methods of dating . . .

The finds: Herod's fortress—extent, luxury, provision for food and water . . .

Story of the fall of Masada: Josephus' account, archaeologists' reconstruction of the events.

Roman army: Tenth Legion, camps, wall, ramp, weapons . . .

Zealot community: intensity of feeling about Rome, mass suicide . . .

Pupils should imagine themselves into the situation of both the Romans and the Zealots, through writing diary accounts, letters, posters for keeping morale up . . .

The symbolism of Masada for modern Israel—'Masada shall not fall again!'
I F 14, 19.

Archaeology—Qumran
The emphasis with this age group should be on the discoveries and the detective work of the experts in different fields rather than on the significance of the religious beliefs of the sect or its relationship to early Christianity.

Story of the discovery of the Dead Sea Scrolls in caves in 1947. Excavation of the 'monastery'. Building and cemetery.

Scrolls: biblical MSS, the community's own literature. Writing materials. The copper scroll—hidden treasure?

Life of the community: vows and discipline, ritual meals and baptisms. Study of the Law.

Archaeological methods: work on the MSS, pottery, buildings . . . Dating, restoration, translation . . .

Problem of identifying the community: Josephus, Philo, Pliny—and the evidence from the site and the scrolls.

Eleven to thirteen year olds can do a more extensive study of the importance of the discoveries for getting nearer to the original biblical writings and for understanding Judaism in the first century.
I F 12, 17, G (b) 17.

Archaeology—Solomon; the Patriarchs
The approach should be similar to that of the above units. The emphasis should be on the light that archaeological discoveries throw on the way of life of people in the past.
Solomon: Temple, stables, copper smelting works at Ezion-Geber . . .
Patriarchs: finds at Mari and Nuzi, Beni-Hasan tomb, story of Sinuhe . . .

How the Bible came to us (see chapters 12 and 13)
The story of the translation and transmission of the Bible can be tackled in a number of different ways, but the main aims will be to allow the pupils to discover both the importance which Christians have placed on the Bible, especially on its being available to ordinary people, and the complexity of the task of the scholars engaged on work on the text.

Possible areas for development:
Biblical manuscripts. This could follow on from finding out about the Qumran scrolls and fragments. Emphases—no originals, only copies of copies. Deterioration of vellum and papyrus. Accounts of some of the dramatic finds, e.g., of Sinaiticus. Over 4,000 complete or partial copies of books of the N.T. in existence. Work of scholars, especially in piecing together fragments.
Translating the Bible into the language people understand. Jesus spoke in Aramaic; the N.T. writers wrote in Greek (even Mark, whose Greek was not very good), so that it could be read outside Palestine; second century Latin translations; Jerome's new Latin translation in the fourth century—the Vulgate (i.e., for the common people). The struggle in the fourteenth and fifteenth centuries to get the Bible into English—for the common people, especially the life and work—and death—of Tyndale. The continuing task of translation. Words change their meaning—charity/ love . . . New MSS may throw light on a passage which has been difficult to translate. Many English versions in the nineteenth and twentieth

centuries—*R.V., R.S.V., N.E.B., J.B., T.E.V.* . . . Some translations made by individuals—Moffatt, Phillips. . . . Work of the Bible Societies—translation and distribution of the Bible all over the world in over a thousand languages . . . Jewish versions of the Bible.

Problems of translating the Bible into another language. Different cultures have different values, customs, etc., and there are often no equivalents in another language. The words 'judge', 'priest', 'shepherd', 'king', 'prophet' . . . meant something quite different to the people of ancient Israel from what they mean to us, e.g., 'shepherd' was a nomad, not a sheep farmer in our sense (see unit 'Shepherd'). Should the words of the Bible be translated into the equivalent words in another language or should the translators use quite different words but try to give the original meaning?

I G (b) 3, 4, 6, 13, 17, 20.

The Church in action—Coventry Cathedral
This serves as an illustration of the approach which could be used in relation to other cathedrals or active centres of the Christian Church.

If possible take the pupils to visit the cathedral, though not without considerable preparation. Coventry Cathedral has an Education Department which prepares materials for use by schools and it organises visits of school parties.

The story of the destruction of the old cathedral and the building of the new one. 'Phoenix rising from the ashes.'

The features and the symbolism of the building—its relation to the shell of the old cathedral, its chapels and what they stand for, the windows, the Bethlehem font, the tapestry, the tablets of the Word . . .

The theme of reconciliation and the activities which express this, especially the relationship with Germany. The cross of nails.

The cathedral's ministry to the city—industry, community relations with people of other faiths, work with children and young people, drama, service in the local community.

The cathedral's worship—its own congregation, tourists, groups who come for special reasons, e.g., to perform a dance-drama . . .

Compare the role of the cathedral with that of the monastery in the middle ages or of the village church before the industrial revolution. Discussion about the function of churches and cathedrals today will be much more valuable towards the end of the study than at the beginning.

This unit lends itself to visual presentation of what the pupils have learnt, especially the symbolism of the building and its activities. IV 2.

The Church in action—Christian Aid

Other organisations which provide help for people in need may well also be studied, but it is particularly appropriate in religious education to discover something about the relief work which is being done by the Christian Church.

The most effective approach for this age group is to focus on one area and study it thoroughly, if possible exploring what the help would mean in the life of one family. Different groups in the class might take a different project each, finding out as much as possible about the region and its people as well as about the help that Christian Aid is giving. If one project comes to life for the pupils they will know much more about what Christian Aid is and what it stands for than if they are given a more extensive and more superficial account of its work.

The Education Dept. of Christian Aid (P.O. Box No. 1, London, SW1 9RB) supplies materials, including filmstrips, for use in schools.

Christmas customs

The aim of this unit is to help the pupils to discover the original significance of the customs that have come to be associated with Christmas— the Christmas tree (an evergreen), the yule log . . . The choice in the fourth century of December 25 as the date on which the Christian Church would celebrate the birth of Jesus . . . This contributes to an understanding of the close relationship of religion and culture, and it also gives the pupils an insight into the complexity of the meaning of Christmas as a deeply significant festival.

Story of the Wise Men

The aim is to help the pupils, through an exploration of the story of the Wise Men in music, literature and art, to see how it has gripped the imagination of men down the centuries, and to help them to realize that the story we are so familiar with is much more elaborate than the original story in the Bible, but that the value of such a story does not depend on whether it actually happened.

The pupils tell the story of the Wise Men, then look up Mt. 2:1—12 and discuss the differences.

Search books of carols and hymn books, make a collection of those which refer to the story, and note the variations.

Look at a variety of pictures—reproductions of old masters, modern paintings, photos of sculptures, stylised pictures (old Christmas cards are a useful source). In small groups discuss the pictures. What do they have in common? In what ways are they different? Possibly choose one example and write a poem which expresses what they feel about it (in blank verse). This may lead on to reading poems which have been inspired by the story. T. S. Eliot's 'The Journey of the Magi' could come at the end of an encounter with the story in its different forms; it could be too difficult earlier.

Explore modern interpretations of the story, e.g., Carl Menotti's 'Amahl and the Night Visitors', if possible learning some of the songs.

Read and discuss Henry Van Dyke's 'The Story of the Other Wise Man'.

Because the story of the Wise Men speaks to man at a deeper level than that of his mind, the pupils should use the creative arts to express what they have discovered about the story and its interpretations.
I G (a) 28.

13—15

The Bible in Christianity (see chapters 12—14)
This can be part of the unit 'Sacred Places' or it can be done later and build on the understanding gained in that unit. Where pupils enjoy R.E. and are already interested in the Bible, it would be possible to tackle it before 'Sacred Writings'.

The aim is to explore the nature of the literature of the Christian Bible, its role in the Church, and its significance for Christians today.
The literature of the Bible.

The O.T.—the Jewish Bible. The three-fold division. The Law and the Prophets were scripture at the time of Jesus; the early Church accepted the later Jewish fixing of the Canon of the Writings. The Apocrypha and the Pseudepigrapha. The Septuagint—variations in translation. Most N.T. quotes from LXX. The Christian use of O.T., e.g., Mt. 2:15/Hos. 11:1; Mt. 3:3/Isa. 40:3. Practical problems of using scrolls.

The N.T.—Epistles written first. Letters to young Churches, wrestling with problems, e.g., 1 Cor., and the Law in Gal. and Rom. Use of traditions about the life of Jesus before Gospels written. Nature of the Gospels. Problem of lost writings, e.g., end of Mark, part of Corinthian correspondence. Pupils should be helped to imagine themselves into the situation of the early Church, not just to memorise facts about the Bible. They should consider the cultural context of the writings—the significance of the political situation and the religious questions of the time.

The fixing of the Canon—fourth century. The disputed books.

Translating the Bible. (Build on 'How the Bible Came to Us'. If the pupils have not done that unit some of the key areas should be included here.) Problems of translating writings which came out of a different culture. Compare different English versions; look especially at interpretations given to certain passages in *N.E.B., The Living Bible* . . .

Interpreting the Bible. Authority, and methods of interpretation in the Patristic period, in the Middle Ages, at the Reformation, in the seventeenth and eighteenth centuries. Biblical scholarship in the nineteenth and twentieth centuries. (This should involve looking at significant examples, not working through a historical study.)

Using the Bible in worship. Significance of the placing of the Bible in Churches. Use of lectionaries. Liturgical use of biblical quotations. How far do these help/hinder the ordinary Christian's understanding of the Bible?

The Bible in the life of the Christian. Different approaches to the authority of the Bible for everyday living. What problems face the Christian layman in the use of the Bible? (Cf. nature and range of the literature, different cultural context, different emphases and teaching in different parts of the Bible, original writings directed to specific situations.) Advantages and disadvantages of daily Bible readings, with/without the guidance of notes.

How does a Christian resolve the tension between the authority of the written word, the authority of the Church which interprets and uses the Bible, and the authority of the Holy Spirit?
I G (a) 2, 17, 40.

Who was Jesus? (See chapters 13—14)
The aim is to help the pupils to discover how it was that the first

Christians came to say about Jesus that he was more than an ordinary man, how they came to use a title like 'Son of God' for him, and how they came to offer to him worship offered only to God.

The first Christians were a group of Jews who, after the resurrection experience, came to think of Jesus in a new way. How would they try to convince their fellow Jews—Pharisees, Zealots? The claim that he was the Messiah, reference to the Scriptures . . .

Use of the material about Jesus—sayings, incidents, miracle stories, parables, passion narrative . . . in preaching, teaching new converts, working out solutions to problems in the Church and in worship.

What differences would there be when they tried to share their faith with Gentiles? Meaning of 'word', 'son of God', 'son of man' . . . in Jewish and Hellenistic thinking. References to Jesus in Paul's letters.

Collections of sayings of Jesus, e.g., 'Q'. Cf. Gnostic sayings from Nag Hammadi.

Eventual creation of the Gospels. Redaction criticism. Documents expressing Christian faith.

N.B. This is one area where it is especially necessary to encourage pupils to take an objective look at their R.E. textbooks. They should be given accurate and objective information, especially about Judaism and the Pharisees, and about the growth of the N.T. writings and they should compare this with what they find in some of the books written for schools. They should also be encouraged to ask (of any book) what the author's aims and presuppositions are and how far these affect his selection and interpretation of material. Inevitably, because R.E. is only slowly moving away from the confessional approach, most books for schools are written from an 'inside' position, and they assume that their task is to help pupils towards a similar position.

I F 1, 15, G (a) 2, 40, 41.

15+

Christian life and thought in 19th and 20th centuries

There are numerous topics which could be included under this heading, but the aim of all of them should be an objective study not an apologetic one. The weaknesses and the failures, the strengths and the achievements should be presented impartially, and the pupils should be encouraged to understand the reasons that lie behind events, developments, attitudes, etc.

It is wise to focus on selected areas in a topic and deal with these thoroughly, using them as illustrations of the topic and setting them in the context of the topic as a whole, rather than trying to cover the whole of a topic superficially.

Problems of philosophical theology

The aim should be to help the pupils to understand the issues involved, and the ways in which different people have tried to find a solution to the problem. It is more important for pupils to learn how to handle the issues than to 'solve' the problem. They may, individually, come to their own provisional conclusions, but none of the problems has a cut and dried solution, and the greatest help we can give at school is the ability to think clearly, to recognise the nature of the questions being asked, and to know in what ways scholars are wrestling with the questions.

This study should be built on units like 'Signs and Symbols', 'Asking Questions' and 'What is Belief?' Where the pupils have not done such units the key areas should be included at an early stage in this sixth form study.

Biblical image themes (see pp.92–3)

These are background units, in which the aim is to help the pupils to understand the way of life which produced the particular image.

For the sevens to nines it will be sufficient to let the children find out what the life of the nomadic shepherd was like. Possibly for the nines to elevens, and certainly for older pupils, attention should be drawn to the significance of the image in religious thinking. However, for top Juniors this should be related to the use of 'bread' and 'water' as images of 'life'; the use by Christians of the images 'bread of life' and 'living water' in relation to Jesus can be understood more easily at secondary level. In the Middle school years and above, the pupils could make lists of expressions which reveal the significance of certain images in our language, and see how these images have developed out of our way of life, e.g., royalty: given a royal welcome, crowned with success, beauty queen, king size, princely sum . . .; the sea: when the tide turns, ebb and flow, shipshape, half-seas over . . .; sport: playing the game, fair play, knock-out, sticky wicket, the ball's in your court . . .

The notes are not in the form of schemes of work. They are indications of the kind of material appropriate to the study of the image. The actual study should include a great deal of imaginative work.

7–9

Shepherd

Shepherds were nomadic or semi-nomadic. Farmers occupied all the arable land and shepherds had to roam the more barren hill country.

A shepherd was with his flock the whole time, day and night (Lk. 2:8). He had to search out pasture and water for them (Ps. 23). He went in front (Num. 27:17) and they followed him with complete trust. They knew his voice and would come when he called (Jn. 10:4).

There were no fields, no fences, no sheepdogs. The shepherd had a sling which he used with great skill. If a sheep strayed too far he put a stone just beyond it to make it come back. He had to defend his flock from attack by wild animals (1 Sam. 17:34–35). If he was close he would use his club; if he was some distance away he would use his sling (1 Sam. 17:40, 49).

If a sheep got lost the shepherd would go and look for it (Lk. 15:3–7). A good shepherd cared for his sheep and would risk his life for them; a bad shepherd would flee in time of danger (Jn. 10:11–13). The prophet Ezekiel described the leaders of the people in his time as bad shepherds (Ezek. 34).

At night the sheep were counted into a fold, and the shepherd would sleep across the opening to protect his flock from danger—wild animals or thieves (Jn. 10:1, 9).

The sheep were so dependent on their shepherd that helpless people were described as 'sheep without a shepherd' (1 Kings 22:17, Mt. 9:36).

Compare the very similar life of nomads and semi-nomads today, e.g., bedouin in Syria and Jordan and the south and west parts of Israel. I G (b) 12, 15, 16.

9–11

Bread

The life and work of the farmer, in contrast to the nomadic shepherd.

Lived within walled village or town and went out by day to work in the fields which were outside the walls (Lk. 15:25).

No fences—boundaries marked by cairns of stones, 'landmarks' (Dt. 19:14).

The ground was stony and stones had to be cleared from the field. Ploughing a straight furrow (Lk. 9:62). Seed was sown by scattering it on the ground (Mt. 13:3—8). Weeds, 'tares', looked like wheat when the plants were young but didn't grow so tall. Harvesting—reaped by sickle, stalks cut near the ears of grain. Threshed by oxen treading it, separating the grain from the husks (Dt. 25:4). Winnowed by tossing it in the air—grain fell to the ground, chaff carried away by the wind. Cf. Gideon having to winnow down in a winepress so that raiding tribes couldn't see (Judges 6:11).

First-fruits of the harvest offered to God (Dt. 26:1—11). Harvest festivals—Passover (barley harvest), Pentecost (wheat harvest).

Bread made daily (Mt. 6:11) because it didn't keep. Unleavened bread did keep so it was used on journeys. Cf. Passover (Exod. 12:8). Effect of leaven (cf. Lk. 13:20—21).

Grinding corn was menial task. Philistine humiliation of the captured Israelite hero, Samson (Judges 16:21).

Grindstone was one of the most important family possessions. A law said that it couldn't be used as a pledge for payment of a debt (Dt. 24:6).

Bread was staple diet. Famine described as 'want of bread' (Amos 4:6).

Bread was always broken, never cut (Lam. 4:4, Mt. 15:36, Lk. 22:19, Acts 2:42).

Water

Four months each year without rain. Former and latter rains (Dt. 11:14, Joel 2:23—24). N.B. Early belief that rain fell when the windows of the heavens were opened (Gen. 7:11—12).

Nomads had to dig for water (Gen. 26:22—23; Gen. 26:15). There could be fighting over possession of wells (Gen. 26:19). Shepherds met at wells (Exod. 2:15, Gen. 24, 29:1—10). Water from different wells was recognised by the taste (2 Sam. 23:13—17). Wells would dry up (Gen. 37:23—24; Jer. 38:6—13). Nomads' life spent in the search for water—oasis (Exod. 15:27), well, river, 'still water' (Ps. 23). Had to know how to make bitter water sweet (Exod. 15:22—25) and how to get water in the desert (Exod. 17:6).

Springs were called 'living water' (Gen. 26:19; cf. Jer. 2:13).

Only small rivers in Palestine, apart from the Jordan, which is at the bottom of a rift. Rivers dried up in droughts (1 Kings 17:1−7).

Drought brought a desperate situation (1 Kings 18:5−6). Picture of desolation (Jer. 14:1−6). When there was famine in Palestine there was always 'corn in Egypt' because of the Nile (Gen. 12:10. Cf. also Gen. 42).

Villages were always built near a water supply. The well was the meeting place for women, who fetched water morning and evening (cf. Gen. 24:11). Three sizes of water pots—for storing, for carrying from the well and for travelling (I Sam. 26:12).

Reservoirs were cisterns hewn out of the rock, or dug and lined with mud brick. They could develop a crack (Jer. 2:13). Water supply was a problem for Jerusalem—excellent site for defence but no well or spring. Watercourse built from spring outside the walls. (This was how David captured Jerusalem—a group entered the city through the watercourse— 2 Sam. 5:5−8.) Hezekiah built a reservoir and a tunnel to carry the water (2 Chron. 32:1−4, 30). Masada—rock fortress, little rain, no wells or springs; rain water channelled into vast underground cisterns.

Israel today: irrigation for all intensive agriculture and horticulture. Dead Sea useless. Transformation of the desert—'blossoming like the rose'. Piped water from the Jordan to the Negev. Cities built in the desert with their water supply piped from the River Jordan.
I F 9, 12, 16, 19, G (b) 9, 12, 15, 16, 19, 20.

11−13

Light

Lighting for houses: poorer houses would have no windows, other houses would have small windows at least six feet from the ground, therefore always dark inside. Clay lamp with wick floating in oil, put on lampstand (Lk. 11:33). Kept burning all night. Needed refilling daily (cf. Mt. 25:1f). Travellers had lantern-like pottery lamp which was carried on a stick (cf. Ps. 119:105). In early days torches were probably wood covered with resin (Judges. 7:16).

Nomads' life was geared to daylight. Lamps and fires gave little effective light out of doors. Darkness was feared. Attacks were made at night (1 Sam. 14:36, Judges 7:9f.). Morning light was welcomed (2 Sam. 23:4).

Light in the Temple: lamp with pure olive oil kept burning before the veil of the Temple (Lev. 24:2). Seven-branched golden candlestick (2 Chron. 13:11). The Titus Arch in Rome shows the candlestick being carried in triumphal procession after the destruction of Jerusalem in A.D. 70. The seven branched candlestick is one of the main symbols of Judaism.

Darkness stood for calamity and despair (Ps. 107:13–14; Isa. 9:2; Amos 5:18; Lk. 23:44).

God, who created light (Gen. 1:3), was described as light (Ps. 27:1; 1 Jn. 1:5). Jesus was also described as light (Jn. 1:4f., 8:12). Cf. also the vision of the new Jerusalem (Rev. 21:23, 22:5).

13–15

Fire

Domestic fires: poorer houses would have a depression in the floor in the middle of the room—no chimney; well-to-do families would have a brazier (Jer. 36:22). Cooking was usually done outside the house.

Much more important in the development of the imagery of fire was the earlier experience of the nation: destruction of Sodom and Gomorrah (Gen. 19:24), Moses and the burning bush (Exod. 3:2), one of the plagues (Exod. 9:23), following the pillar of fire (Exod. 12:21f.), the experience at Mount Sinai (Exod. 19:18), Elijah on Mount Carmel (1 Kings 18:21–39) and on Horeb (1 Kings 19:11–12).

Fire was important in the Temple—fire on the altar for consuming the sacrifices (Lev. 6:8f.).

Gehenna ('hell' in English versions) came to stand for a place of punishment and torment (Mt. 5:29–30). The word comes from Gē Hinnom, the Valley of Hinnom, outside the west wall of Jerusalem. In the seventh century B.C. it was used for heathen practices (2 Chron. 33:6) so it was defiled by King Josiah and it became the city's rubbish dump (2 Kings 23:10), with its continually burning fire and its rotting matter (cf. Mk. 9:48).

Fire could destroy (cf. Josh. 6:24) but it could also purify (Isa. 6:1–7; Mal. 3:2; Zech. 13:9). In either case it symbolised power. Cf. Acts 2:1–3. N.B. The association of wind and fire also in 1 Kings 19:11–12, Ps. 104:4.

15+

Pilgrim People (see p.93)
The aim of this unit is to discover how the image of always being on
the move, having no permanent resting place—and therefore no promised
security and no cause for complacency—arose. There are two main lines
to follow: Israel's early nomadic life, which left its permanent mark on
the nation and its thinking, and Israel's experience through history of
being uprooted.

This should not be a traditional course on the history of Israel, but
should select and focus on events which illustrate the theme.

N.B. The Christian Church's taking over of the image: Acts 7—Stephen's
speech, Jesus' teaching about no security offered to his followers (Mt. 8:20;
Lk. 9:23f.) . . .

Bibliography

This is a 'starter' bibliography. A booklist which tried to provide adequate coverage for the teaching of religious education at all age levels would not only be quite unwieldy, but it could take no account of the books which are continually being published. Further advice should be sought from R.E. Advisers, teachers' centres, the C.E.M. R.E. Advisory and Information Service (C.E.M., Annandale, 2 Chester House, Pages Lane, N10 1PR), Shap Information and Advisory Service (Religious Studies Department, Borough Road College, Isleworth, Middlesex), the book reviews in *Learning for Living,* etc.

An attempt has been made to include only books which can be recommended with some confidence. However, there are frequently reservations to be made about minor points. For example, *The Bodhi Tree* by Greta James ends with a reference to the Buddha foretelling the coming of Jesus, an interpretation which would be quite unacceptable to Buddhists. In a story such as this one the reference can be omitted, but it is possible, especially at secondary level, to make positive use of misleading or inaccurate material in books by helping the pupils to look at it objectively and do a critique of it in the light of what they have been learning.

A rough and ready classification according to price range has been attempted. Pamphlets and small or relatively inexpensive books are marked (S), large or fairly expensive books are marked (L). Those in between, with no mark, cover a price range of approximately £2, except at primary school level where the range is nearer £1.

It is even more difficult to indicate an age range for which books will be suitable. For example, only academic secondary pupils could make extensive use of the text of some books but younger or less able pupils might make good use of the illustrations or of certain sections of the text if they were looking for information on a particular topic. However, in a bibliography to be used by First school as well as sixth form teachers it is important to try to give some indication of the level. This is shown by a figure in brackets. A book marked (9) means that it is probably useful for children of nine years and over. Most of the books in the general sections could be used by sixth formers even though they were written for adults. More advanced specialist books have not been included. Teachers who are sufficiently knowledgeable to use them are likely to know where to find them.

The age range indicated refers to average and above average pupils. There are practically no good religious education books on the market for extensive use by slow learners, and the task of mediation therefore falls to the individual teacher. There are, however, many books from which pupils can use illustrations and small sections of the text.

Many of the books on other faiths which are difficult to get through ordinary booksellers may be obtained from the addresses given below.

Buddhist Publication Society, 5 Heathfield Gardens, London W4 4JU.
Ramakrishna Vedanta Centre, 54 Holland Park, London, W11 3RS. (Hinduism)
Minaret House, 9 Leslie Park Road, Croydon, Surrey, CRO 6TN. (Islam)
Jewish Education Bureau, Sinai Synagogue, Roman Ave., Leeds LS8 2AN.
Jewish Memorial Council Bookshop, Woburn House, Upper Woburn Place, London WC1H OEP
Jewish National Fund, (Education Dept.), Rex House, 4/12 Regent St., London, SW1Y 4PG.
Pam's Sikh Bookshop, 17 Abbotshall Rd., Catford, London, SE6 1SQ.
Sikh Missionary Society, 27 Pier Road, Gravesend, Kent.
Oxfam (Education Dept.), 274 Banbury Road, Oxford, OX2 7DZ.

A comprehensive bibliography on world religions (prepared by the Shap Working Party) can be obtained from the Community Relations Commission, Education Department, 15—16 Bedford Street, London WC2E 9HX.

Audio-visual aids have not been listed. Filmstrip producers are well known to schools, and a list of the photos, posters, records and objects illustrative of the different religions would be endless. Some of them can be obtained from the Jewish Education Bureau and from Minaret House, and slides (expensive but of excellent quality) can be obtained from Bury Peerless, 22 King's Ave., Minnis Bay, Birchington, Kent.

I World Religions
  A Religions and the study of religion
  B Buddhism
  C Hinduism
  D Sikhism
  E Islam
  F Judaism
  G Christianity (a) The Christian Faith and the Christian Church
                  (b) The Bible (c) Issues in religion

II Non-religious systems of belief
  A Humanism
  B Marxism

III Miscellaneous

IV Biography

V Literature for children and young people
  A Fiction
  B Myths, legends and folk-tales

I. World religions

A. Religions and the study of religion

1. Berger, P., *A Rumour of Angels. Modern Society and the Rediscovery of the Supernatural* (Penguin) (S)
2. Bettis, J.D. ed., *Phenomenology of Religion* (S.C.M.)
3. Bliss, K., *The Future of Religion* (Penguin) (S)
4. Bowker, J., *Problems of Suffering in Religions of the World* (C.U.P.) (L)
5. Brandon, S.G.F., *Man and his Destiny in the Great Religions* (Manchester U.P.) (L)
6. Cole, W.O. ed., *Religion in the Multi-faith School* (Bradford Education Committee and Yorkshire Committee for Community Relations)
7. Greene, B. and Gollancz, V., *God of a Hundred Names* (Gollancz) Prayers.
8. Hallencreutz, C.F., *New Approaches to Men of Other Faiths* (World Council of Churches)

180

9. Hill, Janet, ed., *The Homelands of Migrants in Britain* (I.R.R.)
10. Holroyde, P. ed., *East Comes West* (Community Relations Council) (S)
11. Howells, Wm., *The Heathens. An Introduction to the Study of Religion* (Doubleday pbk)
12. Ling, T.O., *A History of Religions East and West* (Macmillan)
13. Neill, S., *The Christian Faith and Other Faiths* (O.U.P.)
14. Norbeck, E., *Religion in Human Life. Anthropological Views* (Holt, Rinehardt and Winstone)
15. Parrinder, E.G., *African Traditional Religion* (Sheldon pbk) (S)
16. Parrinder, E.G., *Worship in the World's Religions* (Sheldon pbk)
17. Pritchard E.E. Evans, *Theories of Primitive Religion* (O.U.P.)
18. Robertson, R. ed., *Sociology of Religion. Selected Readings* (Penguin) (S)
19. Satprakashananda, Swami, *The Use of Symbols in Religion* (Vedanta Society) (S)
20. Sharpe, E.J., *Fifty Key Words in Comparative Religion* (Lutterworth) (S)
21. Smart, Ninian, *The Religious Experience of Mankind* (Fontana)
22. Streng, F.J., *Understanding Religious Man* (Dickenson)
23. Taylor, J.V., *The Primal Vision* (S.C.M.)
24. Thomas, O.C. ed., *Attitudes Towards Other Religions* (S.C.M.)
25. Vogt, E.Z. and Lessa, W.A. eds, *Reader in Comparative Religion. An Anthropological Approach* (Harper and Row pbk) (L)

For pupils
26. Ballard, M., *Who am I?* (Hutchinson) (15)
27. Bridger, P., *A West Indian Family in Britain* (R.E.P.) (13)
28. Carlton, E., *Peoples and Religion* (A. and U.) (16)
29. Carlton, E., *Religions in Society* (A. and U.) (16)
30. Guy, H.A. ed., *Our Religions* (Dent) (16)
31. Hedges, S., *With One Voice* (R.E.P.) An anthology (14)
32. Parrinder, E.G., *A Book of World Religions* (Hulton) (11)
    Parrinder, E.G., *Themes for Living* (Hulton) (16) (S) Anthologies
33.   1. *Man and God*
34.   2. *Right and Wrong*
35.   3. *Society*
36.   4. *Goal of Life*

37. Turner, H.W., *Living Tribal Religions* (Ward Lock) (15) (S)
38. Welbourn, F., *Atoms and Ancestors* (Arnold) (16) (S)
39. Wolcott, L. and C., *Religions Round the World* (Hulton) (10)

B. Buddhism

1. Conze, E. ed., *Buddhist Scriptures* (Penguin) Mainly Mahayana
2. Narada, Thera, *Buddhism in a Nutshell* (Buddhist Publication Society) (S)
3. Narada, Thera, *The Dhammapada* (Maha Bodi Soc. of India) (S)
4. Rahula, W., *What the Buddha Taught* (Gordon Fraser)
5. Rawson, P., *The Art of South East Asia* (Thames and Hudson)
6. Robinson, R.H., *The Buddhist Religion* (Dickenson)
7. Ross, N.W., *Hinduism, Buddhism, Zen. An Introduction to their Meaning and their Arts* (Faber) (L)
8. Saddhatissa, H., *The Buddha's Way* (A. and U.)
9. Saddhatissa, H., *Buddhist Ethics* (A. and U.) (L)
10. Suzuki, D.T., *An Introduction to Zen Buddhism* (Rider)
11. Woodward, F.L., *Some Sayings of the Buddha* (Buddhist Publication Society)

For pupils
12. Cohen, J.L., *Buddha* (Macdonald) (10)
13. James, G., *The Bodhi Tree* (Chapman) (11; written for younger children)
14. Lefever, H., *One Man and his Dog* (Lutterworth) (10)
15. Ling, T.O., *Buddhism* (Ward Lock) (15)
16. Slade, H., *Meeting Schools of Oriental Meditation* (Lutterworth) (16) (S)
17. Sugana, G.M., *The Life and Times of the Buddha* (Hamlyn) (11)

C. Hinduism

1. Ananyananda, Swami, *Essentials of Hinduism* (Ramakrishna Vedanta Centre) (S)
2. Basham, A.L., *The Wonder that was India* (Fontana)

3. Hinnells, J.R. and Sharpe, E.J. eds., *Hinduism* (Oriel)
4. Hopkins, T.J., *The Hindu Religious Tradition* (Dickenson)
5. Isherwood, C., *Vedanta for the Modern World* (A. and U. pbk) (S)
6. Klostermeier, K., *Hindu and Christian in Vrindaban* (S.C.M.)
7. Mascaró, J. trans., *The Bhagavad Gita* (Penguin) (S)
8. Mascaró, J. trans., *The Upanishads* (Penguin) (S)
9. Paramananda, Swami, trans., *Bhagavad-Gita* (Ramakrishna Vedanta Centre)
10. Rolland, R., *The Life of Ramakrishna* (Ramakrishna Vedanta Centre)
11. Ross, N.W., *Hinduism, Buddhism and Zen. An Introduction to their Meaning and their Arts* (Faber) (L)
12. Yatiswarananda, Swami, *The Divine Life* (Ramakrishna Vedanta Centre) (S)
13. Yatiswarananda, Swami, *Universal Prayers* (Ramakrishna Vedanta Centre) (S)
14. Zaehner, R.C., *Hinduism* (O.U.P. pbk)
15. Zaehner, R.C. trans., *Hindu Scriptures* (Everyman Paperbacks)

For pupils
16. Bridger, P., *A Hindu Family in Britain* (R.E.P.) (15)
17. Crompton, Y., *Hinduism* (Ward Lock) (14) (S)
18. Sharpe, E.J., *Thinking about Hinduism* (Lutterworth) (15) (S)
19. Slade, H., *Meeting Schools of Oriental Meditation* (Lutterworth) (16) (S)
20. Yogeshananda, Swami, *The Way of the Hindu* (Hulton) (10) (S)

D. Sikhism

1. James, A.G., *Sikh Children in Britain* (I.R.R./O.U.P.)
2. Kaur, Kanwaljit and Singh, Indarjit, *Rehat Maryada. A Guide to the Sikh Way of Life* (Sikh Cultural Society) (S)
3. McLeod, W.H., *The Sikhs of the Punjab* (Oriel) (S)
4. Mansukhani, G.S., *Guru Nanak—World Teacher* (Sikh Missionary Society) (S)
5. Mansukhani, G.S., *Introduction to Sikhism* (Hemkunt Press) (S) 100 questions and answers
6. Singh, Kurshwant, *Japji* (Morning Prayer) (Sikh Missionary Society)(S)

7. Singh, Shanta Serbjeet, *Nanak the Guru* (Orient Longmans)
8. Singh, Trilochan et al., *The Sacred Writings of the Sikhs* (A. and U.)
9. Sidhu, G.S., *The Sikh Temple* (Sikh Missionary Society) (S)
10. Sidhu, G.S. et al., *In the Guru's Footsteps* (Sikh Missionary Society) (S)
11. Sidhu, G.S. et al., *The Saint-Soldier* (Guru Gobind Singh) (Sikh Missionary Society) (S)
12. Wylam, P.M., *Brief Outline of the Sikh Faith* (Sikh Courier) (S)

For pupils
13. Cole, W.O., *A Sikh Family in Britain* (R.E.P.) (14) (S)
14. Cole, W.O. and Sambhi, P.S., *Sikhism* (Ward Lock) (14) (S)
15. Wylam, P.M., *Guru Nanak* (Children's Book Trust, Delhi) (12; written for younger children) (S)

E. Islam

1. Ali, Yusuf, *The Holy Qur'an* Text and commentary, Arabic and English (Muslim World League, Mecca) (L)
2. Bawany Wakf, Begum A., *Islam, an Introduction* (Al Madina Trust, London) (S)
3. Cragg, K., *Alive to God. Muslim and Christian Prayer* (O.U.P.)
4. Cragg, K., *The House of Islam* (Dickenson)
5. Duncan, A., *The Noble Sanctuary—Portrait of a Holy Place in Arab Jerusalem* (Longman)
6. Grube, E.J., *The World of Islam* (Hamlyn)
7. Hashmi, F., *The Pakistani Family in Britain* (Community Relations Commission) (S)
8. Hollis, C. and Brownrigg, R., *Holy Places—Jewish, Christian and Muslim* (Weidenfeld and Nicolson) (L)
9. Maudoodi, A.A., *The Islamic Way of Life* (Islamic Publications, Lahore) (S)
10. Maudoodi, A.A., *Towards Understanding Islam* (Islamic Publications, Lahore) (S)
11. Pickthall, M.M., *The Meaning of the Glorious Koran. An Explanatory Translation* (Mentor)

12. Shah, Idries, *Caravan of Dreams* (Quartet pbk) (S) Stories, sayings and poems.
13. Shah, Idries, *The Way of the Sufi* (Penguin) (S)
14. Stewart, D., *Early Islam* (Time-Life International) Up to modern times.
15. Watt, M.M., *Muhammad, Prophet and Statesman* (O.U.P.) (L)

For pupils
16. Akram, Mohammed, *Far Upon the Mountain. The Experience of a Young Pakistani in Britain* (British Council of Churches) (15) (S)
17. El Droubie, R., *Islam* (Ward Lock) (14) (S)
18. Iqbal, Muhammad, *The Way of the Muslim* (Hulton) (10) (S)
19. Sugana, G.M., *The Life and Times of Mohammed* (Hamlyn) (11)
20. Taylor, J.B., *Thinking about Islam* (Lutterworth) (15) (S)
21. *Children of the Minarets* (Hutchinson) (9)
22. *Primers of Islam* First, Second and Third (Muslim Educational Trust) (12; written for younger Muslim children) (S)
23. Islamic Correspondence Course Twelve booklets: *Basic Principles of Islam; Muhammad; Prayer; Fasting; Pilgrimage; Poor Due; Prophets of God; Early Caliphs; Moral Teachings of Islam; Qur'an and Hadith; Muslim Holidays and Ceremonies; Essentials of Islam* (Minaret House) (15) (S)

F. Judaism

1. Adler, M., *The World of the Talmud* (Schocken)
2. Baeck, L., *The Essence of Judaism* (Schocken)
3. Brookes, R.S., *A Dictionary of Judaism* (R. and K.P.)
4. Cohen, A., *Everyman's Talmud* (Dent)
5. Davis, M. and Levy, I., *All about Israel* (Jewish National Fund)
6. Gaster, T.H., *Festivals of the Jewish Year* (Morrow)
7. Goldin, H., *Bible and Talmud Stories* 3 vols. (Hebrew Publishing Company, N.Y.)
8. Hollis, C. and Brownrigg, R., *Holy Places—Jewish, Christian and Muslim* (Weidenfeld and Nicolson) (L)
9. Kollek, T. and Pearlman, M., *Jerusalem* (Weidenfeld and Nicolson) (L)
10. Lehrman, S.M., *Jewish Customs and Folklore* (R. and K.P.)

11. Lehrman, S.M., *The Jewish Festivals* (R. and K.P.)
12. Milik, J.T., *Ten Years of Discovery in the Wilderness of Judaea* (S.C.M.)
13. Pearl, C. and Brookes, R.S., *A Guide to Jewish Knowledge* (Valentine Mitchell)
14. Pearlman, M., *The Zealots of Masada* (Hamish Hamilton)
15. Singer, S. trans., *Authorised Daily Prayer Book* (Eyre and Spottiswoode Includes *Ethics of the Fathers*.
16. Spiers, B. ed., *Haggadah for Passover* (Pordes) (S) Hebrew and English.
17. Vermes, G. trans., *The Dead Sea Scrolls in English* (Penguin)
18. Wouk, H., *This is My God* (Collins)
19. Yadin, Y., *Masada* (Sphere)
     A Page From (Jewish National Fund) (S) Jewish sacred writings.

For pupils

20. Ansubel, N., *A Pictorial History of the Jewish People* (Jewish National Fund) (14)
21. Domnitz, M., *Judaism* (Ward Lock) (13) (S)
22. Domnitz, M., *Thinking about Judaism* (Lutterworth) (15) (S)
23. Domnitz, M., *Understanding your Jewish Neighbour* (Lutterworth) (11) (S)
24. Epstein, M., *All about Jewish Holidays* (Ktav Publishing House) (12)
25. Fishman, I., *Introduction to Judaism* (Valentine Mitchell) (13)
26. Palmer, G., *Quest for the Dead Sea Scrolls* (Dobson) (11)
27. Silbermann, A.M. ed., *The Children's Haggadah* (R. and K.P.) (9)

G. Christianity

(a) The Christian Faith and the Christian Church

1. Betz, O., *What do we Know about Jesus?* (S.C.M. pbk) (S)
2. Bowden, J., *Who is a Christian?* (S.C.M.) (S)
3. Bainton, R., *The Penguin History of Christianity* Vols. 1 & 2
4. Bornkamm, G., *Jesus of Nazareth* (H. and S.)
5. Bruce, F.F., *Jesus and Christian Origins outside the New Testament* (H. & S.)
6. Cragg, K., *Alive to God. Muslim and Christian Prayer* (O.U.P.)
7. Dodd, C.H., *The Founder of Christianity* (Fontana) (S)
8. Edwards, D.L., *What is Real in Christianity?* (Fontana) (S)

9. Hastings, A., *A Concise Guide to the Documents of the Second Vatican Council* Vols. 1 and 2 (D.L.T.)

10. Hollis, C. and Brownrigg, R., *Holy Places–Jewish, Christian and Muslim* (Weidenfeld and Nicolson) (L)

11. Jeffery, R.M.C., *Case Studies in Unity* (S.C.M.) (S)

12. Moore, P.C., *Tomorrow is Too Late: Taizé–An Experiment in Christian Community* (Mowbray pbk)

13. Pittenger, N., *God in Process* (S.C.M. pbk) (S)

14. Read, D.H.C., *Christian Ethics* (H. and S. pbk)

15. Robinson, J.A.T., *The Difference in Being a Christian Today* (Fontana) (S)

16. Robinson, J.A.T., *The Human Face of God* (S.C.M.) (L)

17. Sykes, S.W., *Christian Theology Today* (Mowbray pbk)

18. Vidler, A.R., *The Church in an Age of Revolution. 1789 to the Present Day* (Pelican)

19. Vidler, A.R. ed., *Objections to Christian Belief* (Constable)

20. de Waal, V., *What is the Church?* (S.C.M.) (S)

21. Williams, H.C.N., *Basics and Variables. The Future of the Church in the Modern World* (R.E.P.) (S)

22. Williams, H.C.N., *Coventry Cathedral. A Guide to the Cathedral and its Ministry* (H. and S.)

23. Williams, H.C.N., *Coventry Cathedral in Action* (R.E.P.) (S)

For pupils

24. Baker, M., *Christmas Customs and Folklore* (Shire Publications, Tring) (9) (S)

25. Broadberry, R. St. L., *Thinking about Christianity* (Lutterworth) (13) (S)

26. Eve, E., *The Christmas Book* (Chatto, Boyd and Oliver) (11)

27. Fice, R.H.C. and Simkiss, I.M., *We Discover the Church* (Arnold) (8) (S)

28. Grigson, G., *The Three Kings* (Gordon Fraser) (10)

29. Hackel, S., *The Orthodox Church* (Ward Lock) (13) (S)

30. Hichens, T.S., *The Christian Church* Oxford Children's Reference Library No. 15 (10)

31. Hole, C., *Christmas and its Customs* (Bell) (10) (S)

32. Hole, C., *Easter and its Customs* (Bell) (10) (S)

33. Johnson, L.S. ed., *Christmas Stories Round the World* (Warne) (8) (L)

34. Keats, Ezra Jack, *The Little Drummer Boy* (Puffin) (6) Words and music

35. Kelly, P., *Roman Catholicism* (Ward Lock) (13) (S)
36. Leacroft, H. and R., *Churches and Cathedrals* (Lutterworth) (10)
37. McLellan, J., *Days of the Year* (R.E.P.) (10)
38. Palms, R.C., *The Jesus Kids* (S.C.M.) (13) (S)
39. Post, W. Ellwood, *Saints, Signs and Symbols* (S.P.C.K. pbk) (10) (S)
40. Stacey, D., *The Man from Nazareth* (R.E.P.) (15)
41. Stacey, J., *The New Superstition* (R.E.P.) (15)
42. Thomson, G.S., *Medieval Pilgrimages* (Longman) (10) (S)
43. Ward, M., *The Protestant Christian Churches* (Ward Lock) (13) (S)

(b) The Bible

1. Baker, T.G.A., *What is the New Testament?* (S.C.M.) (S)
2. Bowden, J., *What about the Old Testament?* (S.C.M.) (S)
3. Bruce, F.F., *The Books and the Parchments* (Pickering and Inglis) (S)
4. Bruce, F.F., *The English Bible* (Lutterworth)
5. Hayes, J.H., *Introduction to the Bible* (S.P.C.K. pbk) (L)
6. Hunt, G., *About the New English Bible* (O.U.P.) (S)
7. May, H.G. ed., *Oxford Bible Atlas* (L)
8. Sparks, H.F.D., *On Translations of the Bible* (Athlone pbk) (S)
9. Spivey, R.A. and Smith, D.M., *The Anatomy of the New Testament* (Collier-Mac) (L)
10. Walton, R.C. ed., *Source Book of the Bible for Teachers* (S.C.M.) (L)

For pupils

11. Bowden, D., *The World of the New Testament* (R.E.P.) (15)
12. Corswant, W., *Dictionary of Life in Bible Times* (H. and S.) (13) (L) OP but may be in libraries
13. Daniell D.S. and Lampe, G.W., *Discovering the Bible* (H. and S. pbk) (10) (S)
14. Eisenberg, A. and Elkins, D.P., *Worlds Lost and Found. Discoveries in Biblical Archaeology* (Abelard–Schuman) (11)
    Holm, J.L. and Mabbutt, G.C., *Phoenix Series*
15. Book 1 *The Land where Jesus Lived* (7)
16. Book 2 *The Shepherd Boy who Became a King* (8)
17. Book 4 *The World's Best Seller* (10)
    Teachers' Handbook
18. Hood, G., *Festivals* (R.E.P.) (14) Festivals of ancient Near East

19. Jones, C., *New Testament Illustrations* (C.U.P. pbk) (13)
20. Jones, C., *Old Testament Illustrations* (C.U.P. pbk) (13)
21. Lace, O.J. ed., *Understanding the New Testament* (C.U.P.) (16) (S)
22. Mellor, E.B. ed., *The Making of the Old Testament* (C.U.P.) (15) (S)
23. Mowvley, M., *The Testimony of Israel* (R.E.P.) (15)
24. Whanslaw, H.W., *Paper Reeds and Iron Pens* (R.E.P.) (9) (S)
25.   *Dictionary of the Bible* (Collins) (10) (L)

(c) Issues in religion
1. Allport, G.W., *The Individual and his Religion* (Collier-Mac)
2. Barbour, I., *Issues in Science and Religion* (S.C.M.) (L)
3. Carrington, R., *A Million Years of Man* (Weidenfeld and Nicolson pbk)
4. Douglas, M. ed., *Man in Society* (Macdonald)
5. Edwards, D.L., *The Last Things Now* (S.C.M.) (S)
6. Farrer, A., *Love Almighty and Ills Unlimited* (Fontana) (S)
7. Habgood, J., *Religion and Science* (H. and S. pbk)
8. Hick, J.H., *Evil and the God of Love* (Fontana)
9. Hick, J.H., *Philosophy of Religion* (Prentice-Hall pbk)
10. MacKinnon, D.M. ed., *Making Moral Decisions* (S.P.C.K.)
11. Macquarrie, J., *God-Talk* (S.C.M. pbk)
12. Macquarrie, J., *Three Issues in Ethics* (S.C.M.)
13. Moule, C.F.D. ed., *Miracles* (Mowbray)
14. Neill, S., *What is Man?* (Lutterworth pbk) (S)
15. Pappworth, M.H., *Human Guinea Pigs* (Penguin) (S)
16. Paul, L., *Alternatives to Christian Belief* (A. and U.)
17. Pittenger, N., *The Christian Understanding of Human Nature* (Nisbet pbk)
18. Ramsey, I.T., *Religious Language* (S.C.M.)
19. Ramsey, P., *Fabricated Man* (Yale U.P. pbk)
20. Robinson, J.A.T., *In the End God* (Fontana) (S)
21. Stevenson, L., *Seven Theories of Human Nature* (O.U.P. pbk)
22. Thorpe, W.H., *Biology and the Nature of Man* (O.U.P.) (S)

For pupils
23. Donovan, P., *Religious Language* (Sheldon pbk) (16)
24. Goodall, J.L., *An Introduction to the Philosophy of Religion* (Longman pbk) (16)

25. Hull, J., *Sense and Nonsense about God* (S.C.M.) (16) (S)
26. Lord, E., *Mysteries and Problems* (Longman pbk) (15) (S)
27. Maclaren, E., *The Nature of Belief* (Sheldon pbk) (16)
28. Miller, P.F. and Pounds, K.S., *Creeds and Controversies* (E.U.P.) (16)
29. Richardson, R., *The Gods* (Hart-Davis) (14) (S)
30. Richardson, R., *In Love and War* (Hart-Davis) (14) (S)
31. Richardson, R., *Heart and Mind* (Hart-Davis) (14) (S)
32. Richardson, R. and Chapman, J., *Free For all* (Hart-Davis) (14) (S)
33. Young, R.W., *Lines of Thought* (O.U.P.) (16)

II. Non-religious systems of belief

A. Humanism

1. Ayer, A.J. ed., *The Humanist Outlook* (Pemberton pbk)
2. Blackham, H.J., *Humanism* (Pelican) OP but may be in libraries
3. Blackham, H.J. ed., *Objections to Humanism* (Pelican) (S)
4. Hawton, H., *Controversy: Humanist and Christian Encounter* (Pemberton pbk) (S)
5. Hawton, H., *The Humanist Revolution* (Pemberton pbk) (S)
6. Huxley, J., *Religion without Revelation* (Watts)
7. Mouat, K., *What Humanism is About* (Pemberton) (S)
8. Osborn, R., *Humanism and Moral Theory* (Pemberton pbk) (S)
9. Robinson, R., *An Atheist's Values* (O.U.P.)

For pupils
10. Smoker, B., *Humanism* (Ward Lock) (15) (S)

B. Marxism

1. Garaudy, R., *Marxism in the Twentieth Century* (Collins)
2. Gardavsky, V., *God is not yet Dead* (Penguin) (S) Marxist/atheist exploration of Christianity
3. Kamenka, E., *Marxism and Ethics* (Macmillan) (S)
4. Klugman, J. ed., *Dialogue of Christianity and Marxism* (Lawrence and Wishart pbk) (S)

5. MacIntyre, A., *Marxism and Christianity* (Pelican) (S)
6. Marx, Karl, *Selected Writings in Sociology and Social Philosophy* (Penguin) (S)
7. Marx, K. and Engels, F., *Basic Writings on Politics and Philosophy* (Fontana)
8. Marx, K. and Engels, F., *Communist Manifesto* (Penguin) (S)
9. Marx, K. and Engels, F., *On Religion* (Lawrence and Wishart)
10. Ollman, B., *Alienation: Marx's Concept of Man in Capitalist Society* (C.U.P.) (L)

III. Miscellaneous

1. Palmer, G. and Lloyd, N., *A Year of Festivals. A Guide to British Calendar Customs* (Warne) (L)
2. Waters, D., *Book of Festivals and other Occasions for Schools* (Mills and Boon)

For pupils
3. Bell, G., *Signs and Signals* (O.U.P.) (7) (S)
4. Bell, G., What Happens When Series (Oliver and Boyd) (S)
   A Valley is Drowned; A Village Grows; A By-pass is Built; A District is Reborn: A River is Cleansed; An Airport is Enlarged; You Throw Things Away.
5. Bull, N., *Symbols* Books 1—4 (Hart-Davis) (9) (S)
6. Goaman, M., *How Writing Began* (Faber) (9)
7. Harley, E.S., and Hampden, J., *Books: From Papyrus to Paperback* (Methuen) (10)
8. Harverson, P., *Signs and Signals* (Penguin Primary Project— Communication) (9) (S)
9. Knight, B., *Sending Messages* (Blackwell) (9)
10. Lowndes, R. and Kailer, C., *The World of Christmas* (Angus and Robertson) (7) (L)
11. Manning-Sanders, R., *Festivals* (Heinemann) (10) (L)
12. Nketia, J.H. Kwabena, *Our Drummers* (Ghana Publishing House) (9) (S)
13. Opoku, A.A., *Festivals of Ghana* (Ghana Publishing Corporation) (11)

IV. Biography

1. Borrelli, D., *A Street Lamp and the Stars. An Autobiography* (World's Work) (13) (S)
2. Cawte, G., *We Were There. Twentieth Century* (Blackwell) (13) Anne Frank . . .
3. Davey, C., *Kagawa of Japan* (Epworth) OP but may be in libraries
4. *The Diary of Anne Frank* (Pan)
5. Garlick, P., *Conqueror of Darkness* (Lutterworth) (9) Helen Keller.
6. Hodgetts, C., *We will Suffer and Die if we have to. A Folk Play for Martin Luther King* (R.E.P.) (15) (S)
7. Horsburgh, H.J.N., *Mahatma Gandhi* (Lutterworth) (16)
8. Keller, Helen, *The Story of My Life* (Hodder & Stoughton pbk)
9. Kennet, J., *Lilian* (Blackie) (13) Lilian Board.
10. King, C.S., *My Life with Martin Luther King* (Hodder & Stoughton) (L
11. King, M.L., *Strength to Love* (Fontana) Sermons.
12. Mitchison, Naomi, *African Heroes* (Bodley Head)
13. Muggeridge, M., *Something Beautiful for God* (Fontana) Mother Teresa.
14. Norman, D., *Prisoner of the Jungle* (Lutterworth) (12) (S) John Dodd.
15. Parsons, E., *Man against Oppression: Dietrich Bonhoeffer* (Lutterworth (15)
16. Peachment, B., *The Defiant Ones. Dramatic Studies* (R.E.P.) Borrelli, Dolci.
17. Peachment, B., *Down among the Dead Men* (R.E.P.) (13) (S) Sally Trench.
18. Scott, C., *The Pilot who Changed Course* (Lutterworth) (12) (S) Leonard Cheshire.
19. *The Diary, Letters, Poems and Mission of Hanna Senesh* (Valentine Mitchell) (L)
20. *Hannah Senesh: Her Life and Diaries* (Sphere) (S)
21. Shankar, R., *The Story of Gandhi* (Children's Book Trust, Delhi) (14)
22. Slack, K., *Martin Luther King* (S.C.M. Press)
23. Spencer, J., *Workers for Humanity* (Harrap) (14) (S) Vinoba Bhave . . .
24. Target, G.W., *The Nun in the Concentration Camp* (R.E.P.) (13) (S) Mother Maria.
25. Trench, Sally, *Bury me in my Boots* (Hodder and Stoughton pbk) (15)
26. Woodcock, G., *Gandhi* (Fontana) (S)

27. *Stories of Courage* Oxford Children's Reference Library No. 5
     Beethoven, Father Damien, Helen Keller . . . Very brief.

V. Literature for children and young people
(See chapter 7)

A. Fiction The ages given are only a rough guide

4–7

 1. Althea, *Jeremy Mouse* (Dinosaur)
 2. Althea, *Smith the Lonely Hedgehog* (Dinosaur)
 3. Althea, *Smith and Matilda* (Dinosaur)
 4. Carle, E., *The Very Hungry Caterpillar* (Puffin)
 5. Cresswell, H., *The Beetle Hunt* (Longman)
 6. Dickens, F., *Fly Away Peter* (Puffin)
 7. Davies, E., *Little Bear's Feather* (Hamish Hamilton)
 8. Flack, M. and Wise, K., *The Story of Ping* (Bodley Head)
 9. Foreman, M., *Moose* (Puffin)
10. Foreman, M., *Dinosaurs and all that Rubbish* (Puffin)
11. Godden, R., *The Mousewife* (Macmillan)
12. Hoban, R., *A Baby Sister for Frances* (Faber pbk)
13. Hoban, R., *Bed-time for Frances* (Faber pbk)
14. Hoban, R., *The Sorely Trying Day* (World's Work)
15. Hughes, S., *The Trouble with Jack* (Puffin)
16. Hutchins, P., *Tom and Sam* (Puffin)
17. Keats, Ezra Jack, *Peter's Chair* (Puffin)
18. Keats, Ezra Jack, *The Snowy Day* (Puffin)
19. Keats, Ezra Jack, *Whistle for Willie* (Puffin)
20. Keeping, C., *Joseph's Yard* (O.U.P.)
21. Norton, M., *The Borrowers* (Puffin)
22. Piatti, C., *The Happy Owls* (Benn)
23. Ryan, C., *Hildilid's Night* (Longman)
24. Sandberg, I. and L., *Johan at School* (Methuen)
25. Sandberg, I. and L., *Johan's Year* (Methuen)
26. Sendak, M., *Where the Wild Things Are* (Puffin)
27. Shankar, R., *Hari and Other Elephants* (Children's Book Trust,
        Delhi) Indian.

28. Storr, C., *Robin* (Puffin)
29. Strachan, J., *Harriet's Naughty Morning* (Transworld Storychair)
30. Tomlinson, J., *The Bus that Went to Church* (Faber)
31. Viorst, J., *The Tenth Good Thing about Barney* (Collins)

8–11

32. Byars, B., *The House of Wings* (Bodley Head)
33. Hughes, J., *Ditta's Tree* (Puffin) Indian.
34. King, C., *The Night the Waters Came* (Longman)
35. King, C., *Stig of the Dump* (Puffin)
36. Lee, V., *The Magic Moth* (Longman)
37. Lewis, C.S., *The Lion, the Witch and the Wardrobe* (Puffin). And other Narnia books
38. Pearce, P., *A Dog So Small* (Puffin)
39. Pearce, P., *Minnow on the Say* (O.U.P.)
40. Rogers, P., *The Rare One* (Hamish Hamilton)
41. Storr, C., *Marianne Dreams* (Puffin)
42. Storr, C., *Rufus* (Faber)
43. Sutcliff, R., *The Witch's Brat* (O.U.P.)
44. Underhill, R., *Beaverbird* (Puffin)
45. Wilder, L.I., *The Little House in the Big Woods* (Puffin)
46. Wilder, L.I., *The Little House on the Prairie* (Puffin)

9–13

47. Armstrong, W., *Sounder* (Puffin)
48. Bawden, N., *Carrie's War* (Gollancz)
49. Bawden, N., *Squib* (Puffin)
50. Boston, L.M., *A Stranger at Green Knowe* (Faber pbk)
51. Dickenson, P., *The Weathermonger* (Puffin)
52. Durrell, G., *A Zoo in my Luggage* (Penguin)
53. Eckert, A., *Incident at Hawk's Hill* (Hamish Hamilton)
54. Garner, A., *Elidor* (Puffin)
55. George, J., *Julie of the Wolves* (Hamish Hamilton)
56. Godden, R., *The Diddakoi* (Macmillan)
57. Le Guin, U., *The Farthest Shore* (Puffin)
58. Le Guin, U., *A Wizard of Earthsea* (Puffin)
59. Ish-Kishor, S., *A Boy of Old Prague* (Chatto and Windus) Jewish.
60. Korimetz, J., *There, Far beyond the River* (Brockhampton)

61. Melnikoff, P., *The Star and the Sword* (Valentine Mitchell) Jewish.
62. O'Dell, S., *Island of the Blue Dolphin* (Puffin)
63. Serraillier, I., *The Silver Sword* (Puffin)
64. Southall, I., *Hill's End* (Puffin)
65. Southall, I., *Let the Balloon Go* (Puffin)
66. Sperry, A., *The Boy who was Afraid* (Heinemann) Polynesian.
67. Sutcliff, R., *Warrior Scarlet* (O.U.P. pbk)
68. Tolkien, J.R.R., *The Hobbit* (Allen & Unwin)
69. Townsend, J.R., *Gumble's Yard* (Puffin)

11+

70. Christopher, J., *The Prince in Waiting* (Puffin)
71. Christopher, J., *Beyond the Burning Lands* (Puffin)
72. Christopher, J., *The Sword of the Spirits* (Puffin)
73. Hautzig, E., *The Endless Steppe* (Peacock) Jewish.
74. Holm, A., *I am David* (Puffin)
75. Van der Loeff, A.R., *Avalanche* (Puffin)
76. Martin, N. ed., *Here, Now and Beyond* (Oxford English Source Books) Extracts.
77. Pearce, P. and Lucy, B. Fairfax, *The Children of the House* (Puffin)
78. Robinson, J.G., *Charley* (Collins)
79. Taylor, T., *The Cay* (Puffin)
80. Treece, H., *The Dream-Time* (Brockhampton)
81. Williamson, H., *Tarka the Otter* (Puffin)
82. Wrightson, P., *I Own the Racecourse* (Puffin)

13+

83. Dickenson, P., *The Dancing Bear* (Puffin)
84. Golding, W., *Lord of the Flies* (Faber pbk)
85. Hunter, M., *The Stronghold* (Hamish Hamilton)
86. Lee, Harper, *To Kill a Mocking Bird* (Penguin)
87. Livne, Z., *Children of the Cave* (O.U.P.) Jewish.
88. Marshall, J.V., *Walkabout* (Peacock)
89. Martin, N., *Truth to Tell* (Oxford English Source Books) Extracts.
90. Maxwell, G., *A Ring of Bright Water* (Pan)
91. Picard, B.L., *One is One* (O.U.P. pbk)
92. Storey, M., *Pauline* (Faber)
93. Storr, C., *Lucy* (Faber)

94. Southall, I., *Josh* (Angus and Robertson)
95. Tolkien, J.R.R., *Lord of the Rings* (Allen & Unwin)
96. Townsend, J.R., *Hello, Prof. Love* (O.U.P. pbk)
97. Townsend, J.R., *The Intruder* (O.U.P. pbk)
98. Zieman, J., *The Cigarette Sellers of the Three Crosses Square* (Valentine Mitchell) Jewish.
99. Zindel, P., *You Never Loved my Mind* (Bodley Head)

15+

100. Adams, R., *Watership Down* (Puffin)
101. Bolt, R., *A Man for All Seasons* (Heinemann pbk) Play.
102. Camus, A., *Exile and the Kingdom* (Penguin) Short stories.
103.. Camus, A., *The Plague* (Penguin)
104. Evans, J.J., *Guard our Unbelief* (O.U.P.)
105. Garner, A., *Red Shift* (Collins)

B. Myths, legends and folk tales—retold for children

1. Appiah, P., *The Pineapple Child and Other Tales from Ashanti* (Deutsch)
2. Appiah, P., *Tales of an Ashanti Father* (Deutsch)
3. Arnott, K., *African Myths and Legends* (O.U.P.)
4. Barash, A., *A Golden Treasury of Jewish Tales* (Allen)
5. Birch, C., *Chinese Myths and Fantasies* (O.U.P.)
6. Bosley, K., *Tales from the Long Lakes* (Gollancz) Finnish.
7. Choudhury, B.R., *Mahabharata* (Hemkunt Press) Indian.
8. Choudhury, B.N., *The Story of Ramayan* (Hemkunt Press) Indian.
9. Gray, J.E.B., *Indian Tales and Legends* (O.U.P.)
10. Green, R.L., *Myths of the Norsemen* (Puffin)
11. Green, R.L., *Tales of Ancient Egypt* (Puffin)
12. Green, R.L., *Tales of the Greek Heroes* (Puffin)
13. Guillot, R., *Children of the Wind* (O.U.P.) African.
14. Hill, K., *Glooscap and his Magic* (Gollancz) American Indian.
15. Lynch, P., *Knights of God. Tales and Legends of the Irish Saints* (Puffin)
16. McAlpine, H. and W., *Japanese Tales and Legends* (O.U.P.)
17. Narayan, R.K., *Gods, Demons and Others* (Heinemann) Indian.

TEACHING RELIGION IN SCHOOL

The assumption of this book is that the primary aim of Religion courses in school is to give young people an understanding of what religion is, and what it would mean to take one religion seriously. In Great Britain, where the book was written, religious education in the school has most often in the past been concerned with teaching about Christianity primarily. Now there is a concern there to work within a multi-faith situation closer to that in the United States and, therefore, the approach and content herein outlined will be suggestive and helpful to the new programs being developed in this country.

The book is strongly practical and offers a logical structure for teaching the subject at all grade levels. Suggested teaching units and a full bibliography are helpful features of the book.

'To my knowledge we have no book which compares with Ms. Holm's work in relation to the thoroughness and detail with which a practical approach to curriculum for religion in the schools is handled . . . It appears admirably suited for training teachers. . . .'

Professor Norma H. Thompson
School of Education
New York University

OXFORD UNIVERSITY PRESS
ISBN 0 19 913224 0